On the
Good Ship
Hollywood

On the Good Ship Hollywood

John Agar

As told to L.C. Van Savage

BearManorMedia.com

Copyright © 2007 by Martin Agar and L.C. Van Savage
All rights reserved.

Published by:

Bear Manor Media
PO Box 71426
Albany GA 31707

www.bearmanormedia.com

Book Design by Leila Joiner
Back Cover Art © 2007 David Fairrington
(davidfairrington.com)

Printed in the United States of America on acid-free paper

ISBN 978-1-59393-068-4
ISBN 1-59393-068-2

Foreword

On the morning of April 7, 2002, heaven became a little richer, and we on earth a little poorer. On that morning, John Agar Jr., my father and best friend, passed away quietly in his sleep at St. Joseph Hospital in Burbank, California. For those who were fortunate enough to know him, their lives were richer for the experience. I was doubly blessed, not only for knowing him, but for having him as a father, and in my life always. He is buried alongside his wife and my mother, Loretta, at Riverside National Cemetery, next to March AFB.

If you are expecting a tell-all book full of gossip, then you really didn't know this man. Despite all the encouragement from family members and close friends to answer back to things written about him during his relationship with Shirley Temple, he refused. He told me they had agreed never to discuss with anyone anything about their lives together, and he kept his word to the end. This is the only subject I can think of that he wouldn't discuss with me.

John Agar was a man who truly put family first. He adored his wife, Loretta, and would do anything for his two sons and three grandkids, if it were possible. I know one of his great thrills in life was when he, myself, and my son, Ryan, all played golf together. Three generations of Agar's together on the first tee. My son and I both have the same love of the game that my dad did, even though I made the sport of bowling a career choice. (By the way, my father also was quite a bowler, himself.) His one regret was that he never was able to have a relationship with his daughter, Susan. Third parties tried to arrange meetings between them several times, but for whatever reasons not quite known to me, the meetings never happened. I know this hurt him inside very much. In fact, the last phone call he ever made (I had to make it because his eyesight was almost gone) was to Shirley Temple to have her tell Susan to have her eyes checked, because glaucoma is hereditary. This was less than two weeks before he went into the hospital for the last time. Even to the end, Susan was in his thoughts.

This isn't to say John Agar was perfect—far from it. He never hid from his faults and never denied them, as you will read. But he was a man loved by many, and I can honestly say that I have never heard anyone say a negative word about him. Hopefully, after reading this book, you will better know the man I was privileged to call my father and best friend.

God Bless,
Martin Agar

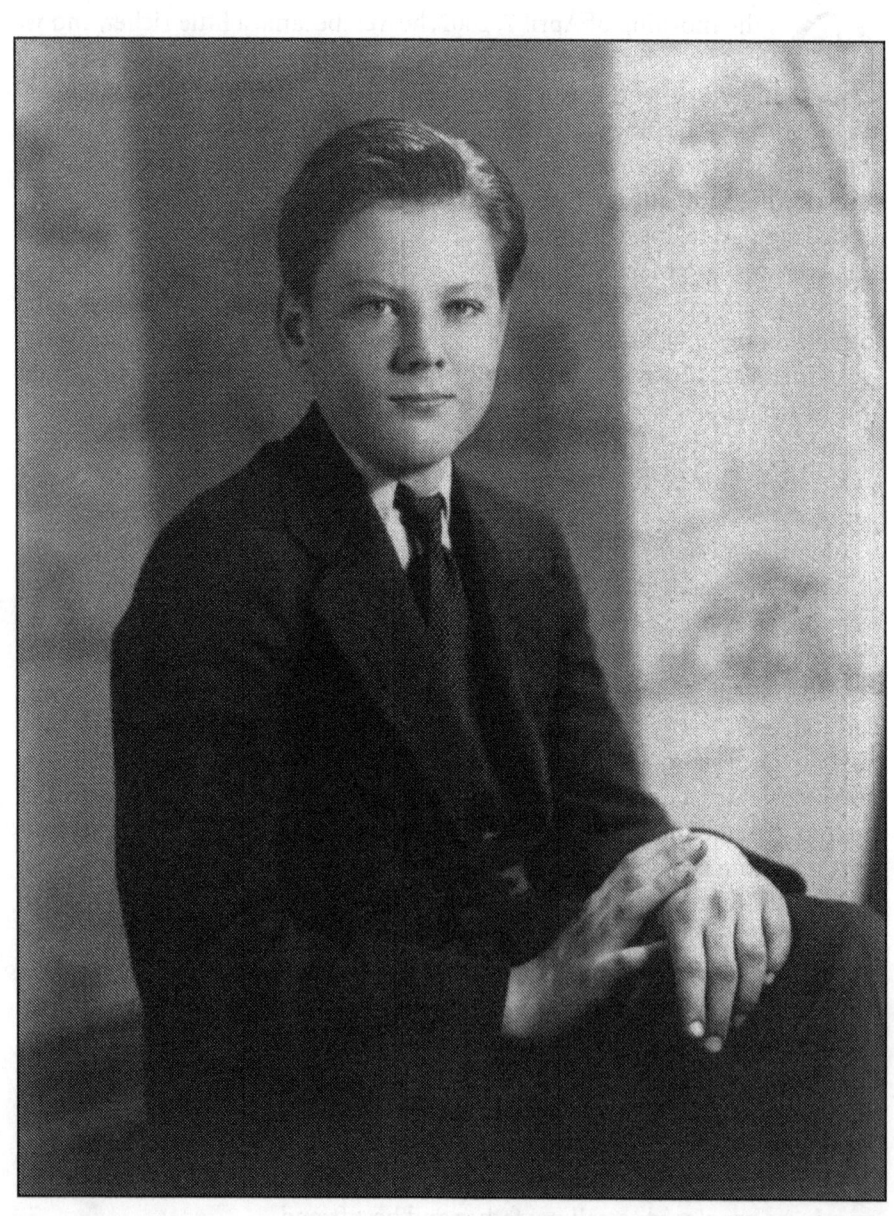

My name is John George Agar, Jr. Named for my father, I was born on January 31, 1921, in Chicago, Illinois. Today, my friends call me Jack—and this is my story.

So many memories come back when you actually (and finally!) sit down and begin to think about putting them all in a book. One of my earliest memories is the sound of those pigs. I'll never forget them. My family owned the Agar Meat Packing and Provisions Company in Chicago, and driving those pigs with a stick into the slaughterhouse was not something I enjoyed, but I did it because it was expected of me. Hearing their screams while they were being slaughtered was terrible for me, horrible. But I was raised to always do the right thing. I could be counted on. I would not always succeed, but it was expected that I would always try my hardest. I always did.

It was a summer job for me, driving those pigs. My grandfather, James Scanlon Agar, wanted me to do it. He thought it would be good for me to know the business from the most basic parts of it on up. It was kind of understood that I'd be going into that business one day, and so he thought I'd better see it all, every aspect of it.

I'd herd those pigs down the street to the slaughterhouse, which was only several blocks from our plant. I had to get up at 4:30 every morning and get a streetcar from our home in Chicago so I could get to the plant in time to do that pig herding. There was a guy there, too, his name was Jimmy the Pig, who would herd the pigs into the slaughterhouse with me. Jimmy always had a huge chaw of tobacco in his mouth that he only removed when he ate.

During that time in 1932, there was a lot of crime around, so the cops used to watch over us as we herded those pigs. I never enjoyed watching how they killed those animals: a rope would be tied to one of their legs, they'd be hoisted up, slit open, and their entrails would fall out, and the men there would clean the pigs to get them ready for human consumption. I hated that. I was devastated by that horror and have never forgotten it. I just could never get used to it. The pigs would scream and squeal so much and so loudly. And, you know, pigs are very smart animals, and I'm certain they knew what was happening. Those are not good memories. For that awful job, I got fifty cents a day. It wasn't bad money for the times, I guess.

It was in the early 1930s, and another childhood memory I'll never forget was the terrible time when the stockyards burned. The fires were burning horribly, and they were coming closer, ashes were flying around everywhere. I remember getting up on the roofs to keep them hosed down. I don't recall being scared, but I was seriously concerned.

And I vividly recall at around age eight or nine when we were in Lakeside, Michigan, where we used to go in the summers. It was right across Lake Michigan from Chicago. I tripped and fell through a glass door and slit open my forearm. I still have a huge scar from it and, oh, did I ever bleed. My maternal grandmother was there, and I guess she made a tourniquet or something, but she stopped the gushing bleeding, and I was rushed to a doctor. After that I got a terrible cut from trying to open a glass window, so, in fact, it's probably a good idea for me to always stay away from glass! I was very lucky. I guess the fates had something more in store for me.

I recall having pleasant summertime memories, too. My parents sent me, when I was eleven, to summer camp in Colorado Springs, where I learned to care for and ride horses. I did pretty well, too, and got good at it and enjoyed it very much. A good thing, because in another decade or so in my life, I'd be riding horses for director John Ford in a still-famous movie called *Fort Apache*. Life sometimes does have a funny way of preparing one for what's coming.

SHE WORE A YELLOW RIBBON (1949)

I attended Harvard Grammar School in Chicago, which was on the south side. When we moved to Lake Forest, Illinois, I went to Lake Forest Academy for a time, but they caught me smoking there and kicked me out. (I hear from that school occasionally, and they always refer to the "year John Agar graduated," but I never did because I was asked to leave.) I'll never forget the day it happened. I was smoking in my room and someone walked in and caught me. I was sent immediately to the principal's office, where I was told that I'd broken the rules and that I was to immediately "get out." No excuses. Just leave. My father had died by this time, and my mother didn't live too far away, even though I boarded at the school, so, in shame, I had to walk home to tell her this unhappy news. I don't really remember her reaction, but I do know she wasn't too tough on me. She was a very loving and caring mother. It was 1936, and I was fifteen and had to spend the rest of that school year in public school, where I really didn't know anyone. It was kind of a hard thing, but I'd broken the rules and that was that. It was then that I learned one plays by the rules in life or one suffers the consequences. I also learned then that it is my job to take responsibility for all the negative things that happen in my life, and I've worked hard to follow that credo. I entered Pauling Academy the next year, where I quickly learned to walk far away from the school when I wanted a smoke! (I do think that some rules kind of beg to be broken.)

At Pauling Academy (I'm on the far right).

I'd started smoking in back alleys with my friends. We'd just smoke our heads off because we were convinced it was a manly thing to do. I surely regret that now, because, after 45 years of puffing on cigarettes and even having been off them for years and years, I'm paying dearly for all those puffs. But more on that later.

My Dad, John, Sr.

I never was a mischievous kid, and I didn't get into trouble much. My siblings and I were expected to always do the right thing and to obey our parents, and so it really didn't occur to me to ever misbehave. I certainly did sometimes, but not often. You know, being raised as I was, it really never crossed my mind to misbehave.

However, I do remember one Saturday when I was around twelve. I'd gone to the movies—with permission from my folks, of course. I was expected to see that movie once and to come home straight afterwards. Well, I didn't. I don't recall the name of that movie, but apparently I liked it so much, I decided to sit through it a second time with my friends. It was very late when I came home, and my father was standing in the doorway when I arrived. Bam! He hit me in the face and knocked me down. I got up and bam again! I went down, and he jumped on me and was slapping me hard. He was livid. I'd never seen him like that. My mother was yelling for him to stop, that he'd kill me, and so he stopped. You can bet that I never, ever disobeyed again. I hasten here to say that my father was a wonderful father, and this was not his habit. He was not abusive, and he didn't hit us. But this time he really nailed me! He had strict rules and expected them to be obeyed and, from his point of view, there was no other choice in the matter. I was his son, he made the rules, and it was my job to obey them, and I surely did from then on. I was never, ever late again. (But, you know, sometimes I think to myself, "Was there something about movies that was attractive on some subliminal level? Why did I take such a chance to enrage my father, just to see a movie?" Were the fates talking to me that day? Well, if they were, I never paid attention to them again while my father was alive. I obeyed him without fail from that time on.) Furthermore, this episode was pretty good training. Later on, when I went into the service, I didn't have to "learn" to obey. It came naturally to me. And then, of course, much later, when I made the film *Sands of Iwo Jima* with John Wayne, we filmed some of it on a Marine base in Camp Pendleton in California, and that early training I had from my parents was evident there

SANDS OF IWO JIMA (1949).

also. Complete obedience! I don't mean to suggest that my parents were like drill instructors, but they would not tolerate insubordination.

I think my parents did a very good job with us. Manners really mattered. We'd better have them and use them. No questions. Whenever someone older than I spoke to me, I was expected to refer to them as Mr. or Mrs. or Miss, even if they told me I could call them by their first names. Now that I'm elderly, I don't have to do that anymore because I don't meet that many people who are older than I, but when I do, they are referred to in that manner. It's hard to change those old and proper customs with people like me, and I don't want to, anyway. I think it is the right and proper and correct way to behave around people.

I did have other jobs as I got older. I remember one when I was about fourteen, where I worked on an army base somewhere near Evanston. I was responsible for cleaning up laboratory stuff. I recall that a young man had died. They decided to open the poor guy up to do an autopsy, and so they did while I was there. Someone had told me they were going to do the autopsy, and I guess I was curious, so I went to see it, and I quickly wished I hadn't. They took parts of that guy to "send away," they told me, and they discarded the rest, and it was up to me to deal with that. I had horrible dreams about that for years and years. It was almost reminiscent of seeing the pigs getting slaughtered, but at least the lab people did pay me five or six bucks a week.

From these jobs I was able to save up enough money so that in 1936 I was able to purchase, with some help from my mother, a second-hand black Ford convertible with a rumble seat in the back. I was fifteen years old, and that car made me feel like I was king of the world. (And the girls loved me, too. I suddenly had an awful lot of girlfriends.) And my love for cars hasn't ever ended. The last car I had to sell was three years ago. It was a '64 Caddy convertible, the one with the fins. A classic!

My Dad, me, Joyce, Mom, brother Jim sitting, and brother Frank Kip.

When I look back on my childhood, I have good memories. My family was strong and loving. We four kids had to mind, be respectful and polite. We were expected to do the very best we could in school and in life, to never hurt another person, and to never say anything negative about others. We were expected to always, absolutely always, do the right thing. It was a tough ethic to live up to, but a good one, and important.

My great-grandfather came to America by boat as a cabin boy from Ireland prior to the American Civil War because he, like so many countless others, wanted to become an American citizen. He settled in Chicago and did well for an immigrant, for it was he who began our huge family industry, the Agar Meat Packing and Provisions Company in Chicago, which became well known for Canadian bacon and ham. The very wealthy Swift and Armour meat packing companies, already in existence, were stiff competition, but my great-grandfather prevailed and the Agar Meat Packing Company thrived. I was proud to be a member of the family that started that business, and I still am.

"Agar," in fact, is a word, a noun, that has nothing to do with meat. Agar is a gelatin-like product of certain seaweeds and is used as a thickening agent for foods. Perhaps somewhere in my genealogy my distant relatives had something to do with a seaweed business, and were called the Agars, the way people were once identified by their trades: Carpenter, Shumaker, Tailor, Cooper, Smith, etc. But it wasn't the seaweed business my great-grandfather became involved with; it was the packing and selling of meats. It was expected that I would go into that business, and I thought eventually I probably would, because my family—my parents, John George Agar and Lillian Rogers Agar, two people I adored and respected—thought I should. But, in fact, I never did go into the meat packing business. Neither my family nor I ever had the slightest inkling I'd end up being an actor, but that's the path I took. I enjoyed it and am delighted to have had that experience.

LITTLE ME.

The very successful Agar Meat Packing Company and Provisions in Chicago was sold in the early 1940s. My beloved father had died of angina, a heart attack, in 1935, when I was only fourteen years old. I still miss him very much. He hadn't even reached his forty-first birthday, and he'd been a wonderful father to my siblings and me. My father was too young to die, and we were all too young to be without him. I'd been born on January 31, 1921, and January 10, 1927 was my adopted sister Joyce's birthday. My brother Jim was born on August 26, 1931 and then Frank arrived on October 10, 1932. (At this writing, they are all still alive and well, and I talk with them on the phone. I wish we could see one another more often, but we're still very close.) But, we were all just too young to have to say goodbye to this man, our father, whom we all loved so.

Even though he died so young, my father still had enough time on this earth to be a very good dad to me, even in the short time we had together. I was able to learn much about life from him, about doing the right thing, about not saying unkind or bad things about people, about working hard and being honorable. I got these things from my mother, too. They taught me well. They both had strong work and moral ethics, and these things have served me well over the years. My father had been an extraordinary guy. He was only 5 feet 8 inches and weighed about 155 pounds, but even with his small size, he became an all-American halfback with the University of Chicago football team, playing under the famous coach, Alanzo Stagg. He also held the world's record for the fifty-yard dash, which, of course, is not run any longer. My father ran that in five and 2/10 seconds! His record was tied, but never broken. He was a terrific athlete. I'm very proud of him.

My mother was only about 5 feet 3 inches, so I come from parents who were neither large nor tall. I've certainly shrunk as I've aged, but my height always was 6 feet 2 inches—much taller than my parents. I've often been asked about my height. I guess I inherited my tallness from my great-uncle Sam. He was 6 feet 4 inches, and his wife, my great-aunt, was only five feet tall and 95 pounds.

That couple had a very interesting life. MGM made a movie, *Blossoms in the Dust* (1941), that was about my great-aunt, Edna Gladney. She founded a home for unwed mothers in Fort Worth, Texas, which was considered very forward-thinking for those years. She was a good woman. She got a law passed in which she demanded that only adults could be called "illegitimate" for having kids without benefit of marriage, but the children in Fort Worth were not allowed to be called that. What a great woman she was. She used to call President Franklin Delano Roosevelt, and he'd answer her. He really did. He'd talk with her, and she'd talk back.

EDNA GLADNEY

After the sale of the meat packing business, my sister, Joyce, two brothers, Jim and Frank (whose nickname was Kip), my mother and I all moved from Chicago, Illinois to Lake Forest (about thirty miles north of Chicago and right on Lake Michigan), and we were already in the new house when we got the news that our father had passed away. My poor, dear mother, who grieved terribly for our father, was thirty-eight years old and suddenly had four young children to support. I was the eldest at fourteen, Joyce was eight, Jim was three, and Kip was two. My father had purchased a life insurance policy worth about $100,000, but when the packing company was sold, my grandfather and great uncles never gave my mother a dime from the proceeds. Not a cent. It's not always easy to forgive those kinds of things. My father had worked very, very hard in the business and, as soon as he died, they cut my mother completely out of everything. And my father had even saved the packing company from going bankrupt during the Great Depression. I guess people have a way of forgetting things like that. My grandfather and great uncles surely did. Perhaps it was because of the insurance policy. I don't know, but even if that's the case, it still wasn't right. Not at all. My mother deserved her portion of that sale. I'll never forget what they did to her when she was most needy.

But my mother was a tough and wise woman, and to this day I have no idea why she did what she eventually did; with the insurance policy and some money that had been invested for her in the stock market by a couple of her uncles, she simply packed up and moved from Lake Forest, Illinois to Beverly Hills, California, in 1943. Even back then, Beverly Hills was a very expensive place to live, but that's what she wanted to do, so she did it. She bought a five-bedroom house that still stands to this day at 613 North Arden Drive in Beverly Hills. She paid $18,500. My mother even had a swimming pool built at the house for everyone to use, and oh, did we love that. World War II was going on, so I was actually in the service at the time she bought that house, but I still remember it well. (She sold that house in 1949 for $49,000. She made a killing!)

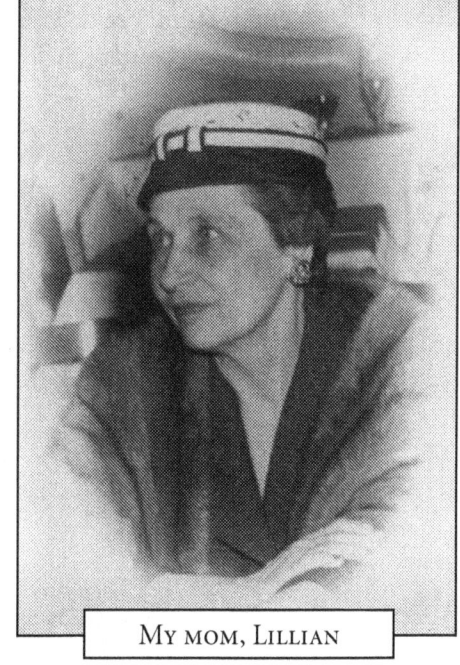

My mom, Lillian

She was able to send me to Trinity Pawling Prep School in Pawling, New York, from which I graduated at the age of 19 in 1940. She wanted all of us kids to have a good education, and so sent each of us to different private schools. (My sister Joyce attended the same school in California, the famous Westlake School, that a fairly well-known young actress also went to. Her name was Shirley Temple.)

Anyway, Pawling Prep was a great experience for me. I learned much there, and have never forgotten my time there. The school closed during World War II, I think, and I regret that other kids couldn't continue going there to get a great education. Math seemed to be my best subject, and I excelled in it. I used to play basketball at Pawling, and football, too. And I was always one way or another involved in track, discus throwing, shot-put, throwing the hammer. Today I would be called a "jock," but that word would have been impolite to use back then. But I *was* a jock, and I loved sports and always have. Golf is my passion now, and I so wish I had more time to devote to it. I think if I could get away with it, I'd golf every day until it got dark. I'll never forget what I heard Ben Hogan say; he hit 100 golf balls every single day with each one of the clubs in his golf bag and that is how he practiced and kept at the top of his form. (By the way, that totaled 1,300 shots a day!) He lived next door to my great-aunt in Fort Worth, Texas, and I remember his coming out here to play at the LA Open at the Riviera Country Club. I was a member when he came. What a thrill! I was amazed to see that man at work. I remember his coming into the club after his round one day. I was there and said, "Well, how did it go today, Mr. Hogan?" And he said, "Oh, I couldn't hit my four-iron." I said, "Well, how well did you shoot?" Par for the pros was 71. He'd shot a 68. He had lunch and then went down and hit four-irons for an hour or so to get it right. He was an awfully nice guy. Remember that horrible accident he had? He was really the comeback kid. But I'm digressing.

PLAYING IN A GOLF TOURNAMENT.

I finished high school in 1940 from Pawling Prep. I never went on to college; World War II fixed that for me. I really had thought a lot about going to Cornell and eventually going on to law school. Everyone was going off to war, and I was eager to do my part, also. I could go to college later, I thought, not knowing then that I never really would. There would be a GI Bill, and I'd get my college education from that, I reasoned, but it was time for me to think about joining up. My mother was planning the move to Beverly Hills, and I wanted to help what was now called "the Cause." I first joined the Navy Air Corps in 1941 in Indiana. We all had to learn everything from a big manual, and then they would take us out to begin the training for flying. We'd fly with a pilot for a certain number of times, and then they'd say, okay, now you have to fly yourself—solo! Oh, I loved it! I soloed five or six times, but then, suddenly and unfortunately for me, the Navy medical men discovered I had an infection in the semicircular canal in my ear, which had begun to severely affect my balance. They would not wait for me to recover, and so my flying career was abruptly ended before it even began. I was given a medical discharge from the Navy Air Corps in 1943, and it was dreadfully disappointing for me. I really had wanted to fly, but what was even more important to me was that I do something productive and helpful for my country and the war effort. My father had served in the army during World War I, and I guess I wanted to do my part, too, as he had. He and my mother taught me a lot about patriotism and the importance of giving back to one's country.

Young people in those days, when training began, were made to understand what it was like to take orders in the service. In wartime there was no room for people who refused to do that. Discipline and tradition were respected. In the early sixties that all changed, unfortunately, even in the motion picture business; the Hays censoring was dropped. Too bad. The Hays Office kept the morals and principals right at eye level. It is a loss to all of us that they don't exist any longer. I guess money is the bottom line now. It seems to be all the film companies are interested in.

And so there I was with that ear problem and unable to serve my country as I'd hoped. I was very disappointed, but realized I had nothing else to do now but to go out to Beverly Hills to live at my mother's home. I even joined the National Guard at this point, and stayed with them for a while.

While I was living in my mother's home, I tried to get into the Army Air Corps. To my great joy, they accepted me, and I was sent to Texas to begin my basic training. I was beyond thrilled. At last, I'd be doing my part. I arrived on Christmas Eve, was given my uniform, and I finally went to bed at 1:00 A.M. At 5:00 A.M., some guy woke me up and said, "Merry Christmas. You're on KP." And so began my Army Air Corps career.

When Roosevelt made the commitment that we would not go to war unless we were attacked, I do believe he knew the Japanese were going to attack Pearl Harbor. It's pretty well documented and, of course, he knew that our going to war would pull us once and for all out of the awful Depression we were still locked into. The war business is a lucrative one. I personally think he made a deal with the Prime Minister of England so that everyone would get after the Japanese. They, after all, were put into a position where they actually had to attack us, and so they obliged us and did just that.

Everyone back then was saying that you had to join up, you had to get into the service, you had to fight for your country, etc. I truly wanted to go. Badly. And now I could! But most of us didn't really have much choice. It was a draft situation after all and, in my case, I was young and unmarried and was therefore a perfect candidate.

And then the war ended. I hadn't even begun! President Harry Truman sent the *Enola Gay* over to Hiroshima and dropped the Atomic Bomb, and that was that. I'd wanted to do my part, although I believed then and believe now that, because of my background, I'd never really be able to kill anyone. But I knew that one can be very patriotic and helpful on the warfront, but not necessarily by doing the killing. There were lots of other important jobs to be done, such as my physical training job, in which I had to keep the men fit by strenuous physical activity. I had to partake, also. I was told by my superior that anything I asked the men to do, I had to do—climbing high walls, swinging from ropes, running, dealing with very rough terrain—the whole thing. I loved it. Athletics has always been important to me. What I didn't much love was, sometimes, during calisthenics, the men, who were supposed to be chanting "one-two-three-four," would chant "SHIR—lie TEM—ple" in time with their jumps, just to see if it would upset me. But I'm getting ahead of myself.

Well, anyway, after that part of my participation in the war effort, I was immediately taken from my job as Physical Training Instructor with the Army Air Corps, and was sent up to Washington State to Bulldozer School, of all things. I had to learn how to use bulldozers because my assignment, I was told, was that I'd be sent to Japan to help clean up the mess the war and the bomb had left behind. I went to Washington, took the training, and was getting ready to be sent to Japan, but was suddenly returned to California, because my mother's father had a very serious problem. He had fallen downstairs and died soon thereafter. I was given a quick leave of absence. Happily, during that furlough, I learned that anyone who'd served for 2S years would not have to go overseas, so all of us who were sent to learn how to operate bulldozers were sent back home. This was good news. I had a little more time to serve, so I went on to Salt Lake City, Utah for a period of time and then went back home to California. I never saw combat, but I would have gladly helped my country had I had the opportunity.

My mother, Lillian Rogers Agar, was now firmly settled in Beverly Hills, and all my siblings were there, too. She proceeded to open up a small clothing boutique on Sunset Boulevard, which did very well. (Just as a little coincidental aside, my future second wife Loretta and her good friend Eileen Forentino actually modeled in my mother's store. I never knew that until years later. Small world.)

My mom and I.

After she sold the house, my mother moved to Palm Springs and opened another boutique, which also succeeded. She could do anything! She kept that shop going until 1971 until she became ill. One day, she slipped and fell; my brother Kip took her back to Texas with him to live with his family, where she finally died on May 7, 1972. I still miss her very much.

I have many fond memories of Beverly Hills and all the California experiences. I remember getting on a train in Indianapolis, so I could get to California, and I think the trip took about three days. When I got off that train in Los Angeles, California, I could hardly believe my eyes. Palm trees! The air was so warm and soft, so unlike the air in Chicago. I was pop-eyed. It was just so beautiful to see. I never expected anything like it. My mother picked me up and drove me out to the house, but I couldn't stop staring at the terrain and the sights, all so completely new to me. I'd certainly read about California, and had heard about it, but being there for the first time was like arriving in Paradise.

Lillian

My mother had become very good friends with a wonderful actress named ZaSu Pitts. ZaSu was so comical, but was most famous for her hands. When she began acting in the early years of the 1900s, she just didn't know what to do with her hands. She felt so awkward about them, and it was a big problem for her. But ZaSu finally figured it out. She began to use her hands in awkward ways on purpose. She made them flutter and float about her while she delivered her lines in a vague, airy way, and the whole thing was just hilarious. ZaSu became very famous for that and was in great demand as a comic character actress. Everyone, audiences and friends alike, just loved her.

One Sunday, when I was in the service, my mother asked me if I'd like to go out to ZaSu's home in Brentwood for the afternoon. I didn't have anything else to do, so I agreed. It happened that ZaSu lived right next door to the Temples, Gertrude and George, and their three children, two boys and a young girl, who was named Shirley. She came over that afternoon, and I remember meeting her then, thinking she was very cute, but really just a little kid. She was about fifteen, and I was around twenty-two at the time. Much older!

People have asked me so often in my life if I had this big sort of shock or explosion in my brain when I first met Shirley. Was I struck dumb when she walked into the room that day? No. I mean, I'd always admired her for being so talented. All of America admired her. After all, she was just a little tiny kid, and she could memorize long, involved tap dance numbers, she could sing, act, cry and laugh on screen, and she was adored by everyone who saw her. Mothers tried to make their little girls look like Shirley. So I was no different from anyone else when it came to seeing her unique beauty. I'd seen her movies, of course—who hadn't?—and I knew she was a beautiful and gifted girl. But no, that day I didn't feel like fainting just because we were in the same room together. I remember that we talked a little bit, and I think some time later we went to a movie, but then I had to get back to my base. We corresponded with each other, and quite soon we began to be romantically involved. I will admit to being occasionally amazed that a famous movie star and I were getting close, but she was young and so was I, and like young folks since the start of time, we fell in love.

And so I began to date Miss Shirley Temple. Imagine—me—John George Agar from Chicago, Illinois, dating the most famous person in America, the young actress President Roosevelt himself had once labeled as the little girl who'd brought America out of the Depression. Sometimes, when I thought about it, I was a little surprised at what was happening to us, but I was falling more and more in love with Shirley, and so her fame just didn't seem to be important.

We wrote to one another while I was away in Spokane, Washington at Bulldozer School. I guess we fell in love, too, in our letters. I got a ten-day furlough over Christmas of 1944 and got to see a lot of her during that time. And it was on one of those furloughs that I asked Shirley to marry me, down on one knee in the old-fashioned way. I also asked her father for her hand in marriage, and he reluctantly agreed. After all, his daughter was only sixteen. Gertrude wanted Shirley to wait until she was 20, but Shirley had a lot of her mother's stubbornness and said absolutely not, she wanted to be married to me when she was seventeen. And that's what happened. And besides, I'd already given Shirley a 2S-carat square-cut diamond ring, which, after promising her mother she would keep it a big secret, she immediately wore to a luncheon for the graduating class of 1945, so she could show the other teen-aged girls.

I don't think Gertrude Temple was a "stage mother" in the terrible and negative sense of the word. She wasn't cruel to Shirley, but she did certainly control her daughter's destiny. She had wanted her daughter to be an actress since before Shirley was born and began training her from her first breath on. And because Shirley was a big investment for her (and for Shirley herself, too—the Temples made certain that Shirley's money would be awaiting her when she was old enough), Gertrude was very right to wonder how I'd support my new wife, because I really had not ever had a "real" job yet, and I must have looked like a pretty poor prospect for her beloved daughter. She made it very clear to me that Shirley would not be getting any of the vast amounts of money she'd earned until she was twenty-one, four years away from that time, and, even then, it wouldn't all come to her in a big lump, but in varying amounts. Fifty-percent of everything she earned, until she was 21, would be set aside by the courts. I didn't pay much attention. I knew I'd find a way to support my wife, and I wasn't particularly dazzled by the "big money" that would come to Shirley at 21 or any age, for that matter. And that is absolutely true.

WITH SHIRLEY TEMPLE

We were in love and just didn't care about all those details. We knew we'd be okay financially, just the way all young people in love know and don't think much about the dangers of the future. I guess, looking back, we should have been more careful or thoughtful about things. But who does that when they're very young and in love? No one, really. I guess it's normal to be blind to the dangers awaiting us all, or we'd never take chances or get married or anything.

Shirley had kept her childlike looks—she was tiny and sweet; as a matter of fact, she still is very youthful looking today. I began to take her to movies and to dinner, and we got along very well. I was very aware of her youth. I mean, we were dating seriously, and she was only sixteen. But she'd led a rather different life from most young girls of the day, and so she really had a maturity about her not seen in other teenaged girls. She was enchanting and wonderful company, and so, after she said yes to my proposal, Shirley and I became husband and wife on September 19, 1945. The wedding was fabulous.

Shirley was a determined little woman and had always insisted that she wanted an old-fashioned wedding, and that, just because she was so famous, her wedding would not turn into a three-ring circus or a "Hollywood circus," as she called it. My best man was a friend from the service. Only about five-hundred of the Temple's and Agar's nearest and dearest were invited to see Shirley and me being married in the Wilshire Methodist Church. It was a pretty spectacular wedding, and Shirley looked simply beautiful. Much has been made about her dress. Lots of pictures were taken, and I'm in most of them just staring down in astonishment and love at my tiny, perfect bride. I think the train of her wedding gown must have been longer than ten feet. She looked heavenly, wonderful, and as she floated down the aisle toward me I thought I couldn't possibly be more in love. I remember thousands of pink flowers and the wedding march. I wore my dress Army Air Corps uniform. (I was a Sergeant then, a buck Sergeant.) It was a wonderful occasion and when it was over I remember we exchanged a very long kiss, which brought much laughter from the people in the church.

After the ceremony, we walked out of the church to be showered with enough rice to feed a small country. And there, awaiting us, was a mob scene, a terrible, awful thing, and *en masse* they began to push toward us. I knew I was marrying someone wildly famous, but I never expected this to happen. It was very scary, and the lights flashing really all but blinded me. I guess Shirley was used to those flash bulbs popping off because, after all, she'd been facing that sort of thing all her life. She just stared at the crowd, leaning hard against me, never blinking at those awful lights. But I wasn't. I was afraid we were going to be trampled to death, so I grabbed my new wife and pulled her back inside; we were saved, for the moment. It was pretty horrible. Getting back to the limousine, so we could get to the reception at the Temples' home on Rockingham Road, was no easy trick. We had to make a run for it, and I recall a lot of the bridesmaids were injured, having their dresses ripped by the throng of people.

The reception was wonderful. There was the traditional cake—fabulous, of course, it would have to be for Shirley Temple!—and there were champagne and toasts, all the things that make up a wedding. And, of course, there were thousands of fabulous gifts, many of which arrived at the reception, the remaining having been sent to the Temples' home before the wedding. We could have opened a store.

After the reception, Shirley changed to a beautiful outfit, I stayed in uniform, she threw her bouquet, and off we went. Lots of other typical glitches happened that day, but we made it finally to our wedding night at the Bel-Air Hotel, and it was a joyful, sweet, and happy time for us. Our honeymoon to Santa Barbara (gotten there again by limo) was far too short because I had to return to Kerns, Utah for military duty, and Shirley went back home to live with her parents until I could return.

We would spend our married life on the Temple grounds, living in the famous Playhouse that Shirley had played in as a child, but which was now converted into sumptuous and livable quarters for us. The famous collection of dolls from the dollhouse was in the basement of the Playhouse, so at least I didn't have to see them all the time. I mean, it was enough that I lived with Shirley; I was not interested in living with a few thousand replicas of her! I believe that huge collection of dolls that had been sent and given to her all her life is now in a museum somewhere. I've often wondered how Shirley felt as a child, when she wandered about amongst all those dolls, all looking back at her, many looking exactly like her. They were not all Shirley Temple dolls. It was an amazing and varied collection from everywhere in the world. And let's not forget that the Playhouse had a projection room so children could watch movies, and there was a bowling alley, too, in the backyard, I think, plus other similar playthings so necessary for a child to have growing up.

At first, though, Shirley and I rented a place in Brentwood, not far from her parents' home. It was right near a golf course. But soon we moved into the renovated Playhouse. The Temples' home was fifty yards away from the Playhouse, and we had to share a driveway (so they always knew when we were coming and going), and it wasn't easy being so close to Gertrude, who was a very controlling woman, to say the least. I was raised to never say anything negative about anyone, and so that's all I'll say about her. Shirley used to go over to her mother's house frequently when we were married, and surely Gertrude came to our home, where she was welcome, but the Temples didn't visit us as often as Shirley visited them. Eventually, I tried to talk with Shirley about one day having a home of our very own, but we had a business manager, a partner of Shirley's father George, who managed a lot of people's money, including ours. All the money I made with Selznick went directly to George and his partner to pay the bills and all. I really don't know if Shirley's money went there or to her parents to manage.

I'd come home. The war was over and I was back home with Shirley. We were planning our lives, but in fact I didn't really have anything much planned. Definitely no job! And I surely had no intention of going back into the meat packing business, but I did have options, and we were exploring them. I was even considering going to Harvard Business School. We had much to plan. Shirley was under contract with David O. Selznick when we got married, although her career at that time was not what it had been. It had slowed considerably. Not that many films were being offered to her. America was not about to forgive Shirley Temple for growing up.

People have asked me a lot of questions over the years about my marriage to Shirley Temple, and I really don't want to go into any great detail about it, but one question that does come up a lot was how my military buddies reacted to my being married to her. I don't recall them ever calling me "Sergeant Temple," although guys in the military do have a habit of doing things like that, but if it happened at all, I know they meant me no harm. I was called "John Temple" a lot, but that kind of thing happens in Hollywood when a non-famous person marries a famous person, and you just have to roll with it. People who get their egos all bruised over that kind of thing are really just foolish.

ME, SHIRLEY, AND DAUGHTER LINDA SUSAN

But even though I had no job, I did have prospects. One night Shirley and I had gone to a party together during a furlough I had earned, and the great movie mogul David O. Selznick was there. We'd met for the first time at our wedding reception, and I recalled that he'd been kind of staring at me. He came up to me and said, "Well, now that the war's over, what are you going to do with your life when you get out of the service?" I told him I hadn't given it too much thought yet, but that I realized I had to begin thinking about making some plans. He said, "Have you ever considered acting?" I said I had not, and that was really the end of that conversation, and I didn't give it much thought. But after I got back to the base, I received a letter from Selznick. In it, he told me he'd like to give me a screen test, and that if he liked the results, he'd sign me to a seven-year contract starting at $150 a week, getting paid forty weeks a year, and if I worked more than that, I'd get paid for that also. So I wrote back and said, "Okay, I'll try it." Well, it really was a pretty nice offer, considering I was at that point making $80 a month. I was pleased at the thought and took the screen test. I remember being very nervous about that. It was to be a scene from *The Farmer's Daughter*, a famous movie that starred Loretta Young. I had to learn some lines and do the scene. That was hard. I'd never acted before. Never.

I guess Selznick liked me, because he eventually signed me after I got out of the service, and I joined the ranks of movie actors. But I saw that screen test, and I really thought it was terrible. Awful! Did Selznick want me on the payroll because I would be a big draw as Shirley Temple's husband? He was a canny guy, very smart and very tuned in to making his movie business a financial success, so I have to say that he was probably not terribly dazzled by my screen test. He probably saw some potential in me, I guess, but maybe more financial potential in having "Husband and Wife team, Shirley Temple and John Agar starring in…" up on posters and marquees. I guess I did okay, because my very first movie would be *Fort Apache*. That still plays on TV all the time.

SHE WORE A YELLOW RIBBON (1949)

I started to take acting lessons with some other new people in the business. We'd study diction and how to walk and stand and move. Everything. We'd go onto a back lot where other young actors under contract would stand; the camera would be behind us, and we'd throw lines to them. It was there I learned how to hit your mark, how to do eye lines (that means that the eyes will always look as if they're looking into the eyes of the person one is acting against, even if there's no one there—and frequently there isn't), and how to never look into the camera, even when it's right under your nose! I really began to enjoy learning all that stuff. I began to think I could possibly become an actor.

Did Gertrude Temple like the idea? No, she didn't, but she wasn't an easy woman to please, anyway, so I really couldn't let that hold me back. Shirley wasn't thrilled with the idea of both of us being in the same business, but she was used to a pretty good lifestyle, and I will admit that I, too, enjoyed the good life—and that takes money. I now had some way to make some, and possibly a lot, if all I was seeing was true. And it was. I soon realized that one could get pretty rich being an actor.

It was the first part of 1946 when all of this happened, and I began to try to learn my new "trade." I studied acting with future famous actors like Rory Calhoun, Guy Madison, Louis Jourdan, and Rhonda Fleming. When I say "with" these actors, I mean that they were also taking acting classes. We were learning together, and the experience was wonderful. I remember during the numerous screen-tests we continued to make that they'd shoot us over our shoulders, throwing lines to us and filming our reactions and answers. This is how we learned how it was to be on the set. We learned action and diction, and those sorts of things, and I found I began to enjoy it more and more. I was discharged from the service on January 29, 1946, and, because of Selznick, I would be employed. My dreams of Harvard and anything else was

gone forever, but I thought then that the tradeoff was a good one; I'd be in the movies.

A year later I was at RKO studios in Culver City, and Selznick was out on the same lot that day with John Ford. My mother and sister had gone to Hawaii on a cruise just before this, and on the boat with them on their return trip was Ford, his wife Mary and their daughter Barbara. My mother met them and, when they landed, I met the Ford family. It was a week after that that David Selznick told me at RKO that Mr. Ford wanted to see me, and that perhaps he had a role for me. I went to see him, and I'll never forget that Mr. Ford had me standing at attention, doing a right-face, a left-face, an about-face, and he had me saluting. "Were you in the service?" he asked me. I said, "Yes sir, I was. I was in the United States Army Air Corps." John Ford looked at me for a minute and said, "Oh, you mean, 'Off we go, into the wild blue yonder?' Crash!!" I laughed and said, "Well, I guess you're right, Mr. Ford. By the way, were you in the service?" "Yes," he said proudly. "I was. I was a Commander in the United States Navy." I looked back at him and said, "Oh, do you mean, 'Anchors Aweigh.' Sink!!" And he laughed. You know, Mr. Ford was thought of as a cranky guy, short-tempered and not much fun, but I never found him to be that way. I could always kid with that man, and he never minded. We had a great relationship. That day, he told me he was getting ready to make a movie which was originally going to be called *War Party*, but when it was released it was renamed *Fort Apache*.

We shot *Fort Apache* in 1947, where I was introduced to Henry Fonda and John Wayne. Shirley starred in this film, also. It was filmed up in beautiful Monument Valley in Utah, where the four corners of four states meet: Utah, of course, Colorado, New Mexico and Arizona. It was breathtakingly beautiful there. Still is, I hope. Pretty thrilling stuff for me, a nobody in the business as I was, appearing with these famous heavyweight actors. I was appearing in a movie being directed by one of the most famous men in all filmdom. (The year before John Ford had shot *My Darling Clementine* there and had built the fort which was used again in *Fort Apache*.) The actors in *Fort Apache* were (and the movie's billing read), John Wayne, Henry Fonda, and Shirley Temple. Then came the character actors' names, George O'Brien, Victor McLaglen, Dick Foran, Ward Bond and Irene Rich (who played my mother) and Anna Lee. What a cast! Then after that in the billing came, "And introducing John Agar." I'm still filled with amazement when I think about all that, even though so many years have passed. I'd grown up seeing these folks in the movies, you know, and so appearing with them in my first movie made me feel really scared. I mean, these actors were famous, very experienced, and this was my first film, and all I'd had was a year of diction, voice and acting lessons, which I'd discovered to my delight that I thoroughly

JOHN WAYNE, SHIRLEY TEMPLE, HENRY FONDA AND ME IN *FORT APACHE* (1948)

enjoyed. But "scared" doesn't even begin to describe how I felt in the presence of these famous, seasoned actors.

I won't forget the day I had to show up on the set for the first time. Shirley didn't go that day to Monument Valley, because her scenes would be shot by a double. (She would play Henry Fonda's daughter in the film, and my love interest.) I went by train, my stomach in knots as it moved along. John Wayne was actually going to be on that train! We both boarded at the same time. He introduced himself, as if I had to be reminded of who he was, and we shook hands (I remember his being taller than I was by a few inches), and he couldn't have been nicer. He was so helpful to me always, as was everyone else on that movie, but it took me a long time to get over my nervousness. Henry Fonda wasn't on the train that day, but I met him later on at the hotel in Monument Valley where we'd all be staying, and he, too, couldn't have been more kind to me. I guess I was just in awe of all of them, and I couldn't get over how nice they were to me.

I'd had my uniform fitted for the movie, and knew all my lines and was ready to go. Lucky for me that I had had that experience back in Colorado Springs when I was 11, so I did know how to care for and ride a horse very well. Just before shooting began, Mr. Ford had sent me to his ranch in Encino, where he had a mare. She was wide and had a spine that stuck straight up and out of her back, and I had to ride her bareback! That was dreadfully painful. I would come home from one of those ordeals, and when I'd get ready to take a bath I'd find my underwear stuck to me—by my own blood. I'd bled from that awful spine on that awful mare! I told the man who was training me, a Mr. Jack, what was happening, and he said, "Go to the drugstore and get some sea salt and put it into the bath water, and that'll help you." I recalled that when I'd played basketball as a kid that I would soak my feet that way, so I thought nothing of Mr. Jack's suggestion. I put the salt into the bathwater, stepped in and sat down and, oh, the pain. I screamed! I complained to dear Mr. Jack, but too late, he'd already told everyone on the set, and they laughed and laughed about it. Very funny. Really. It *was* funny. I can't believe I was so dumb! The saddles on those cavalry horses were called McLellan saddles. They had an opening in it, and I guess Mr. Ford thought an experience on his mare would prepare me for those saddles.

While I can't remember in great detail how it was on the first day of shooting on *Fort Apache*, I think I recall the first scene I was in was when the cavalry was all assembled. As everyone knows, movies are rarely made from A to Z; actors frequently film the ending well before the beginning, and so on. It isn't easy keeping your "attitudes" and personal personalities all in order when you skip around in the story. Mr. Ford (I really think I never did call that man by his first name) would rehearse you and, if you did it right,

SHE WORE A YELLOW RIBBON (1949)

he'd say, "All right, we'll shoot it now." If he didn't like what you did in rehearsal, he'd surely tell you to not do it "that" way, but to do it "this" way, and you'd better do it "this" way or else! If he liked what he saw, you were fine. If he didn't, you'd have to shoot it again and again until you got it exactly the way he wanted it.

John Ford never went to look at the "rushes." Rushes are the pieces of film shot the day before, and they're looked at the day after. (Or at least that's how it was done back in "my" day.) Mr. Ford would never let the actors or actresses see the rushes. If something was technically incorrect, Ford knew exactly what to do, exactly what was on that screen. He would allow the technicians to see the rushes, however, but Ford was a man who made all his shots count. He didn't take dozens of shots from dozens of angles the way they do today. You know, it's almost impossible to not know a John Ford movie when you see it, even if you haven't seen the credits beforehand. The man had such a unique style, his shots were clean and strong, with much depth to them, vividly sharp, and each frame sent some emotion or thought to the viewer. He was demanding, but fair and tough. He had a good sense of humor, and we got along famously. Mr. Ford must have liked me personally and as an actor, because he hired me the very next year to appear in *She Wore a Yellow Ribbon*.

I was lucky enough to become good friends with the actors on *Fort Apache*, in particular Duke Wayne, and I still feel honored being "allowed" to

ME, JOANNE DRU, AND JOHN WAYNE FROM
SHE WORE A YELLOW RIBBON (1949)

call him Duke. He was a great guy. I don't want to give the impression that we were great buddies or best friends. We were very friendly, however. Don't forget that the actors on this movie were much older than I—some of them more than fourteen years. I did then and will always regard Duke Wayne as a big brother to me. And he gave me great acting tips. All the people in the cast were more than helpful.

JOHN WAYNE, ME, SHIRLEY TEMPLE, HENRY FONDA IN *FORT APACHE* (1948)

Sometimes, actors and actresses rave about other actors because they have this need to "take care of their own," or something. Nobody's that perfect! But John Wayne remains one of my heroes. He was a true gentleman, a good man, fair and gentle. But he was a man's man, loved the company of men and could be rugged and rough when he wanted to be. And oh, how he could drink. All those rumors about him were true. An alcoholic? Well, I guess that depends on your definition. Duke would get roaring drunk and could party all night with all his cronies on the movie, who would get even drunker, but, amazingly enough, in the morning, when one might think these men—I was included in all of this, by the way—would be so hung-over and bleary-eyed they couldn't work, they would arrive on the set, costumed and made up and ready to roll. The very instant the cameras began to roll, Duke Wayne and Ward Bond and all the others hit their marks and became instantly sober. I'd never seen anything like that. They knew their lines, they stood and rode tall, and they did their jobs. The minute the director yelled that it was time to quit for the day, the gang would head out to the nearest saloon (although there weren't many places to go partying in Monument Valley) with me in tow, and would start it all over again. They all could drink lakes of liquor, but Duke Wayne could drink more than anyone. He had two hollow legs and a hollow arm, too, I think. This drinking with the boys thing went on with future movies I made with them, and it was really something. We really got roaring drunk. I will admit that I drank way too much with those guys, and it became a problem for me as my life unrolled. A big one.

Thus ended my first film experience. It went quickly. John Ford didn't waste time, and any movie he made would get done fast. I don't recall how fast *Fort Apache* went, although I do remember it did go very quickly. (The next year Mr. Ford shot *She Wore a Yellow Ribbon* in twenty-eight days. Imagine!) Back then, when you were on location, you could shoot six days a week, with Sundays off.

Imagine having as your first film one that would become so famous and such a classic, and to work with those actors and be directed by John Ford. Not many actors get to start out at the top like that. I felt very blessed. This is very gratifying to me. I had a wonderful time making that film.

When the movie ended, we couldn't have a party or anything because Mr. Ford forbade drinking and partying, knowing it could ruin a film. (I don't think Duke and the others paid an awful lot of attention to that edict, although they never got drunk around Mr. Ford or the movie set. Just elsewhere!) So at the end we didn't have a big brawl of a party.

At that point, my salary went up to $300 a week. Shirley was making around $5,000 a week. I was still on salary after *Fort Apache* and so, before my work began on *She Wore a Yellow Ribbon*, I worked on another film with Shirley called *Adventure in Baltimore*, with Robert Young. This was before his TV show *Father Knows Best* and his later, really wonderful series called *Marcus Welby, MD*. Robert Young was a really nice guy, good to work with; he was a great, great actor, and I learned a lot from him. Shirley was again my love interest, and she was also Young's daughter in that movie.

Shirley and I had been married around three years when we made that movie. Things were going pretty well in our marriage—or so I thought! People have asked me over the years if I thought maybe Gertrude was saying negative things about me to Shirley, and I can't honestly answer that. I just don't know. I do know that she was always anxious to have her daughter close by her. After all, Shirley was her golden goose, and Gertrude had invested a tremendous amount of time and money in her daughter. She wasn't about to give it all up just because her golden child had gotten married.

Star in the Dust (1956) and painting by David Farrington shown at the 2ND annual Roy Rogers/Dale Evans Western Film Festival in 1999.

I'll never know if Shirley's two brothers were neglected by the Temples because of their sister's huge fame. The older son, Jack, eventually became a member of the FBI, and George, Jr. went into professional wrestling. Now *that* really upset Gertrude! A lot. But Shirley was very supportive of her brother. But something happened to George along the way—I'm not sure if it had to do with the wrestling or not—but he became a paraplegic and had to spend the rest of his life in a wheelchair. (This happened after my divorce from Shirley.) I did like her brothers very much, however, and they seemed to like me, too.

On January 30, 1948, the day before my birthday, Shirley gave birth to our only child, a daughter, Susan, who immediately became the very light of my life. Shirley has made a statement, in her own book, that I was not present at the hospital when Susan was born. That is untrue. I *was* there. For reasons I'll never know, she said that in print, and I guess aloud, but it just wasn't the truth. I was absolutely, positively at the hospital when Susan was born. Thus, I was happy to be finally contributing something to our life together. I'd been

WITH MY GRANDFATHER, FRANK ROGERS

worried about that and knew I had to start making a living doing something. While Gertrude Temple and other people thought that my being in the same business as Shirley was a big mistake, I had discovered quite by accident that I really loved to act. I still do! I rationalized to myself that there was no reason why I should not be permitted to pursue something I enjoyed and was fairly good at just because I'd been all but handed the opportunity. No one got all excited and upset when other actors got quickly and easily into the movies from other avenues, but because I was married to America's Sweetheart, people resented the fact that I got into films so rapidly. Well, so be it. And, in fact, I began to really get noticed by people in the business. I even had fans. This was difficult for Shirley, I know, because I was emerging as an actor and she was now sometimes being called a "has-been" at the ripe old age of nineteen, and I know that hurt her. She had contributed so much to America and the whole world. She had helped people immeasurably by making them laugh and feel happy during the terrible years of the Great Depression, and well after that. Millions of mothers of little girls tried to make them look and sound and behave like Shirley. She was a miracle in the movies and now, because she'd had the audacity to actually grow up, get married and to become a woman, and because she really could not look and should not act the way on screen that she did when she was three years old and completely adorable, the world turned away from her. To me, she was still adorable, but they turned away from her—many of her former fans, and certainly the studios. A fine thanks that was. It was very hard for Shirley.

The drinking thing was pretty bad for me. I just don't handle booze very well, and, sure, Shirley saw that I was drunk a lot and that couldn't have been easy for her. Shirley was very angry with me. I know she was. That's not easy for anyone to live with, and alcohol has always been a problem for me. I just cannot handle it. I guess I began to drink to excess because of the divorce, but I probably began drinking heavily when I was hanging around with John Wayne and that gang, especially on weekends when we were filming *Sands of Iwo Jima*. But I refuse to blame anyone else. I'm the one who drank. No one forced me. It was my fault that I began, and it's been my fault every time I've fallen off the wagon. I take all responsibility for it. Shirley accused me of being involved with a girlfriend of hers, which was just not true at all. Absolutely, positively untrue.

And I know I drank a lot because I caved into the pressures of having her family so close, so always there. I always felt controlled and not free to make up my own mind about my own life and home and wife. Basically, it was like having to live in the same house with them. Once again, it wasn't their fault that I drank—but I drank because of them and the pressures they put me under, to a point. There were other reasons, too. I got caught a number of times driving drunk, and I know that affected my career, too. I was arrested and convicted of driving under the influence in 1951, and when that happened, David O. Selznick dropped my contract because, he said, I was violating my contract, in which I'd promised to stay out of trouble and, in essence, not embarrass the studio.

I would like to say (and I know I sound vindictive and whining, but I do not mean to) that had I been a huge star like a Barrymore or an Errol Flynn or a Spencer Tracy, my drinking problem would have been covered up. After all, those guys would just trash entire bars and hotel rooms and really hurt people, but the studios would come along behind them and mop it all up, clean it all up, pay people off, make all the repairs and keep it all a secret, because those guys were big moneymakers for the studios, and so it was a wise investment for their little "escapades" to be made to disappear. I wasn't a big enough star for them to bail me out, so they didn't, and I lost my contract. I wasn't worth keeping. Life for me was a mess, and I was making that happen. I myself. Ironically, later on, I heard that Mr. Selznick was drinking heavily himself, so it was bitterly amusing to me that he dropped my contract and took away my livelihood when he had the same problem himself. Did everyone know he drank, too? Maybe.

Maybe we all don't think enough about the dangers of the future. I guess, looking back, we should have been more careful or thoughtful about things,

BIG JAKE (1971)

but who does that when they're very young? No one, really. It's normal to be blind to the dangers awaiting us all.

I came home one night and someone met me at the door, an attorney, and he handed me some papers and said, "Here. Shirley is going to divorce you." That cold. That quickly. Right in the doorway of my own home. Well, basically, it was not my own home—it was the Temples' home. We lived there because Shirley and Gertrude wanted us to. I was stunned at this. I couldn't even get in the door. I was not allowed to go inside to get anything, although later on I was allowed to come back to get my belongings. I was very humiliated, but I knew it was my fault, completely. I knew it. I was desperately unhappy and hurt and embarrassed, but knew I couldn't blame anyone but myself. And so with my tail between my legs, I went back to live with my mother in her home in Beverly Hills. I never heard one word from Shirley. Years later, when I read that she had contracted breast cancer and gone public about it, had recovered and done so much good by telling people about her problem, thus taking it out of the closet, I wrote her a letter telling her how happy I was for her. She did not respond. I guess I never expected her to, but I did want her to know how pleased I was about her recovery, and how impressed I was by her bravery.

Fortunately, I never had to go to court with Shirley. I remember that we had to wait a year for the divorce to be final, and final it became. This all started in the latter part of 1949, and our divorce was completely final in the latter part of 1950. I just woke up one day, and I was divorced.

Today, I am proud of Shirley Temple Black. She has done much with her life and was able to overcome the "America's Darling" thing and show the world that she was an intelligent and productive woman. I always knew she was bright, even though people really always thought of her as just this adorable kid. She went deeper than that. I regret that our marriage couldn't survive, but she went on to marry Charles Black and has remained happily with him over the years. I married my Loretta, so things worked out just fine. I do

LORETTA AND I AT THE GOLDEN BOOTS AWARDS AFTER RECEIVING FIRST EVER AWARDED "LIFETIME ACHIEVEMENT AWARD"

wish, however, that I'd been allowed to know my daughter. It's far too late now, I know, and the thought never leaves me that she's never been a part of my life.

After our divorce, Shirley would go to Hawaii. It was there she would meet the man she is still married to today, Charles Black. I always sent our daughter, Susan, birthday gifts, but they were never acknowledged. When they came back to California, they lived in Coldwater Canyon close to Beverly Hills for a while, and I'd drop over occasionally to try to see Susan, without much luck. I loved our little girl very dearly, but she was to be denied me.

I won't forget the occasion of her sixth birthday. I went over to Shirley's home to give our daughter a birthday gift. Shirley answered the door and told me that Susan was asleep, and she was very tired from all the birthday celebrations she'd been enjoying. I said, "Well, that's fine. I'll leave the gift and will call her later." The door shut and I left. That night, true to my promise, I called and Shirley answered the phone. I asked if I could please speak to little Susan, and she said, "Well, wait a moment," and she went to get Susan. I could hear the Blacks in the background. Finally, my beloved, dear little daughter came to the phone, and I was stunned to hear her say, "Yes, Agar?" Agar. That hurt me so much. It was terrible. I wished her a happy birthday, and she said, "I'm so sorry that I couldn't see you today, but I was so exhausted from all the parties I'd been to." That didn't sound at all like words a six-year-old child would use, but I told her that I understood.

Shortly after that, the Black family moved to Beverly Hills proper. Charles Black adopted my child, and that was that. You may wonder why I allowed him to adopt my child and to give her his name. When my second wife, Loretta, and I adopted our second son, who was born in Glendale Hospital, I received a subpoena, and in it Shirley said that if I did not allow Charles Black to adopt our daughter Susan and let her have his last name, she would take me to court. Well, Loretta and I could not afford that, we just didn't have the money to fight a court battle. I had to agree. But, I reasoned to myself, after all, Susan and I could still be friends, could we not? I was still her biological father. I decided that even though she would become Susan Black, we would still be able to be father and daughter. It was not to be. I was never permitted to see her again and, at this writing, it's been more than fifty years. I still miss my little girl very much.

Eventually, Susan (who I'd always called "Linda Susan" when she was little) met a man when she was in Italy with her mother. (As everyone knows, Shirley got very involved in politics and world affairs.) Susan married that man. She was almost thirty years old, and they had a daughter named Theresa. Susan and the man from Italy eventually divorced when they were in America. Susan and Theresa began living with Shirley and Charlie Black in

(I think) Woodside, which is near San Francisco. I would have loved to have gotten to know my granddaughter, but that would be denied me also. I did try once to get in touch with Susan, and we chatted briefly on the phone, but it was awful and it hurt, and I never tried again. Life isn't always fair.

It was 1950. My divorce from Shirley was final. I was making movies with people I admired and liked, and I was turning my life around.

I'd never given up my membership in the Riviera Country Club. Golf had become a serious passion with me, one that has stayed with me always. I love the game and have loved it since I was six years old. My father used to take me to Lakeside, Michigan in the summers, which is right across Lake Michigan, and there were golf courses there. Dad used to enjoy playing, and he wanted me to like the game, too. I absolutely loved the game then and love it now. I even played often with George Temple. We got along very well, George and I did, and we especially liked to play golf together. Eventually, I got my handicap down to a three! I remember once, in a 36-hole golf tournament, I shot a 76 and my opponent shot a 70. The next day, he shot a 78 and I shot a 71. I beat him by one shot! I won the whole tournament and got a big trophy and everything. A really happy day for me.

My golfing buddies and I got so good at golf that we formed a sort of "club" called The Hackers, and we'd play all over California for charities. We'd make money for them, and that was some fun. We even played in Arizona and other states, too. Golf heaven!

Anyway, after my divorce from Shirley, I went to the club to play some golf. Larry Springer, who was often my golfing partner, was there. He asked me to come over to his house because he wanted to introduce me to a beautiful young actress/dancer named Loretta Barnett. (She later told people that when she first met me, she thought I was way too young. She'd reasoned that if I'd been married to the very young Shirley Temple, I had to be very young myself!)

Oh, Loretta was a gorgeous lady. I could hardly take my eyes off her. We began to talk. I found out that she'd been a background dancer in the very famous movie *Citizen Kane*. And soon, we began to date. Loretta liked to play golf, too! That was really great. Imagine, a beautiful, wonderful young woman, attracted to me, and a golfer, too. I felt like I'd gone to heaven! She didn't play

LORETTA

all through our marriage, but she played enough to make me happy. I remember about six or seven years ago when many of the old Western stars all got together at Long Pine; we played nine holes that day. Great and wonderful fun, that was. Loretta hadn't played in about twenty years, because she'd been so involved in real estate, but she did pretty well that day. She loved to tap dance with friends too. She was "some fun," as they say today. Everyone loved Loretta. We had a wonderful marriage.

Loretta had been married once before, as I certainly had, but we were both free when we met, thank heaven. We began to go out together, to movies and dinners and stuff like that, and then, one evening as we were having a few drinks, I finally proposed to her. It was a very happy moment for me when I heard her say yes. We went straight to the airport, flew up to Las Vegas to get married. (We did not want a big wedding, with a lot of fuss.) There was one little glitch that night; the man who was to marry us thought I'd had too much to drink, and so he objected to doing the ceremony. I guess he thought I'd wake up in the morning and regret what I'd done. But no way! Eventually, we convinced him we were serious and in love and would always feel that way about each other, so he relented and married us. It was May 16, 1951. We spent our wedding night in Las Vegas and flew home the next day.

I don't recall if we called everyone and told them, but I assume we did. Her family accepted me. Louella Parsons got the story first, or at least Louella's version of it, that Loretta had turned me down when I first asked

LORETTA WHEN SHE WAS IN *CITIZEN KANE* (1941)

her to marry me. That wasn't so, but Miss Parsons wasn't all that keen on knowing or reporting the whole truth. For her, the story was the thing. But, then, she reported that we'd gotten married.

Loretta and I stayed at my mother's home (she'd moved out to Westwood), and then we rented a second-floor apartment in Beverly Hills. Right down the street from us lived Jim and Blanche Davis. Jim played the father, "Jock," on the famous nighttime soap, *Dallas*. We became great friends. They had a daughter named Tara. Blanche would bring her around in her baby carriage, and she'd cry out to me, "Papa Jack! Papa Jack!" Oh, she was just the cutest little kid, and Loretta and I adored her. But, horribly, when she was seventeen, she and her boyfriend were both killed in a car accident. It just destroyed Jim. Tara was their only child, and she was the light of their lives. A horrible and senseless tragedy. Loretta and I and a lot of friends went over to the house when we heard the terrible news. Jim was so distraught, so completely shattered, so we all got together in another room and said, "We have to find something for him to do. We have to help him through this and help him take his mind away from it." Well, no one can ever stop remembering a dreadful thing like this, but our hearts were in the right place. So, later, I called John Wayne's office and talked with his secretary, Mary. Mary told me that Duke was off the coast of Mexico on his yacht, and she gave me a number to call. I called him, right on his yacht, and told him what had happened to the Davises. Duke said, "You call Mary right now and tell her to call the director of my new film. I'll be starting work on it soon, and tell him to get a part for Jim Davis in that movie!" Jim got the part, and it really helped him a lot. I can't take credit for that, really. It was Duke who did it. Not I. He was a kind man and had compassion for his friends.

Loretta really tried hard to get me to stop drinking and, after I was married to her for about three years, I finally went into AA and got the help I needed. I went cold turkey. I wasn't a man who drank in the mornings or anything like that, but the social drinking was really my downfall. I have never had the capacity to drink. I don't want to blame genetics for my problem, because the drinking is completely my fault, but I did have relatives who could not tolerate it. My paternal grandfather was widowed and moved to live with his oldest daughter and son-in-law in Montclair, New Jersey. He used to drink an awful lot, and they would water it down for him in an attempt to keep him from getting so drunk. The man lived to be 82, so I guess it didn't damage him.

I remember when I was 12 or 13 years old, living on the southside of Chicago, one of my young friends somehow got a bottle of liquor. I drank a lot of it, we all did—and it was terrible! It made me very sick. When I was in the service, I drank occasionally, but never on a daily basis. My body couldn't handle it. Never! I have always thought I've had a terrible weakness for booze, meaning that I just could not handle it. Other people, our friends, would drink along with me, and it would not alter their behaviors at all. Not me! I'd get stinking drunk on the same amount of liquor. It wasn't fair! I'd be so drunk, and everyone else would be just fine.

So, I finally joined AA and, with a few small exceptions (I'll admit I've slipped once or twice), I've been sober since. Over the years, I've been asked if John Wayne "taught" me to drink. I guess no one has to be taught, but he *was* some drinker. And, of course, I was honored to be his friend, even though he was so much older than I, and I expect this had something to do with my wanting to keep up. I mean, who could have imagined that I, a nobody from Chicago, would be hanging around with America's most famous movie heroes? I loved it. I was happy with those guys. I felt honored and privileged to be allowed to hang around with them. But no one, absolutely no one, forced me to become an alcoholic. I managed to do that all by myself.

I remember one Saturday night when we were shooting *Sands of Iwo Jima*, and we went to a bar. It was supposed to close at 2:00 a.m., and the owner and his wife asked us to come over to his house. We all kept drinking and drinking, and I finally left around 4:00 a.m. I remember looking back over my shoulder at Duke Wayne. He was really knocking them back, and I shook my head in disbelief. He had an appointment at 8:00 a.m. with some of the officers on the base to talk about the movie, but at eight o'clock the next morning, four hours later, Duke Wayne was there and ready to roll! He was married, too, during all this. He had a few kids, and these Wayne kids loved their father very much, and even now never have anything but the nicest things to say about him. They love him still and are working to keep his memory alive.

Loretta and I were living at Studio City when I began to go to AA. I remember one guy there very well. He was a real tough guy, but he was my mentor. He was also an actor. I became friends with him and other members, and some of them were golfers, so we'd all go to our meetings three or four times a week, and then we'd all go out and play golf.

Loretta was a social drinker and never had a problem with alcohol at all. She could take a drink or not. It didn't seem to be a big priority for her. And she continued to drink even when I was in AA, because the people in AA tell everyone that it's the real world to see people drinking, and no one should hide the booze from drinkers. They'll have to get used to the sight of it—just never touch it.

But the drinking had caused me to lose my employment back in 1952, when Selznick fired me for getting arrested for DUI. I didn't have an income for a while, so I began to make independent films. I had an agent, and he got me parts in B movies. I wasn't happy about that, but at least it gave us enough money so we could make it. And Loretta was still modeling at Sax Fifth Avenue, so we did have two paychecks coming in. We were far from wealthy, but we were at least paying the bills. I made B Westerns and, in 1951, made *The Magic Carpet* with Raymond Burr and Lucille Ball, who, I think, was pregnant in real-life with her daughter during filming. Lucy and her husband, Desi Arnaz, were on the brink of creating their show, *I Love Lucy*, and, because of its popularity, they would eventually take over RKO. She was wonderful. I really loved working with her and was so impressed with her business acumen.

WITH PEGGY CASTLE IN *LAWMAN* (1960)

I also worked in *Shield for Murder* (1954) with Edmond O'Brien, who was a lovely, nice man. He played the bad cop in this movie, and I played the good cop. Lots of fun. I continued on making B movies, and it was okay, because I do love to act, but it surely did not make Loretta and me very rich.

On the subject of agents, I had one when I was under contract with Selznick. I really didn't need one, but people probably told me I should have one, and I was so green in that business that I just went ahead and got one. I changed agents, and the next one I kept for a while, then dropped, and then the next one didn't work out either! I really went through them. One guy I had really didn't do me any good. He really didn't get me any jobs. He had become involved with Blanche Davis. Blanche herself became an agent after the death of their beloved daughter, and so Blanche was my agent for a while. Eventually, I got yet another agent, but he, too, didn't get me any work. It seemed pretty hopeless. Any work that I got was because someone wanted me to be in a film. They were all small roles, but at least I was working. Suffice it to say, I don't have an agent now and never will again.

But even today, now that I'm over 80, I will get offered small parts, cameos and things and, if my doctor says I can do it, I always will. I keep hearing

WITH MICHAEL LANDON ON THE SET OF *HIGHWAY TO HEAVEN*

WITH LORI NELSON IN *REVENGE OF THE CREATURE* (1955)

about scripts that people want to offer me, always for small parts, but that's okay because I don't have the stamina for a full-length feature film. I have often talked about my love of acting, and it is so true. I'd act every minute for the rest of my life, if I could. But my emphysema is getting worse. I still work out on a treadmill a couple of times a week, but I always have to have my oxygen near me. It's hard for me to write any longer because my hands shake from old age, and I'm way too skinny, but the spirit and the flame are still strong inside of me. Those things will never be diminished!

I was doing all kinds of things back then, in the movies, mostly B films. (I used to be kind of ashamed to say that, but today the B movies are very popular, and sometimes they're called "cult movies," whatever that means, and "campy," again, whatever that means!) All through the 1950s, I was doing mainly Westerns, such as *Along the Great Divide* in 1951. In the mid-'50s, I'd begun to do science-fiction films. (I know I'm skipping over an awful lot of films as I write this, so will give a complete list at the end of the book.) I really enjoyed making those films a lot: *Tarantula* and *Revenge of the Creature* in 1955, *The Mole People* in 1956, *The Brain from Planet Arous* and *Attack of the Puppet People* in 1958, and *Invisible Invaders* in 1959. Western films and dramatic films were interspersed with those movies. I had made up my mind a long time before that I'd never be walking up on stage to collect an Oscar (actually I never even joined the Academy), and I'd never see any films I was in "breaking all box office records." They paid the bills for us, however, and I loved acting so much, it really didn't matter. I just wanted to be a working actor.

I got a job offer for a movie in Haiti, *The Golden Mistress* (1954), which was about scuba diving. Any kind of athletics has always fascinated me, and this was a new form I could learn. I was taught how to breathe with the aqualung equipment on, and I really enjoyed doing that. I am pretty sure that the aqualung had just been invented about that time, so I guess I can say I was a pioneer, of sorts.

I had one little thing to overcome before I began that film, however. I'd been eating about a quart of ice cream a day, and my weight had really ballooned up. You wouldn't think it to look at me now, but I was pretty heavy. I'd gone to about 216, and I had to get rid of that weight. So after I'd been offered the part, I worked out like crazy at the gym for five or six days a week and dropped my weight down to about 195.

So off Loretta and I went to Haiti. She'd been hired by the studio to put make-up on all the Haitians; she really loved that job, and they loved being made up. We stayed at a hotel that had a swimming pool, which was where I learned to scuba dive.

The movie had a dramatic opening. There was a sunken vessel off Port Au Prince, about 40 feet down. There were a number of large holes in the deck. The underwater photographer thought it would be a very dramatic scene if I were to appear from the prow of the boat, coming into the light and then disappearing back into darkness. I said okay, so we went down, and where I entered the boat was about 30 feet to the prow, but suddenly I couldn't get any oxygen. I didn't panic, but turned and made my way back to where I'd entered. I went up and up, and found I had less pressure on me than I had before, and then I found that I did in fact have enough oxygen. I eventually got to the top after swimming that 70 feet.

There was another incident in that film. We decided to go to an area between Haiti and the Dominican Republic. There was a lake there, and we were still working with the Haitian people. It was their custom, when a loved one died, to cover them with gems, precious stones, and bury them in the ocean. So, in my role as a diver, I was supposed to search for those gems. We shot the scenes in this huge lake instead of the ocean. I vividly recall, as I was swimming way beneath the surface of the lake, seeing large, dark still forms nearby, all around me. I got to the shore and said to the others there, "What the heck were those things?" They answered rather casually, "Oh, those? They're alligators." Nice of them to tell me first! Alligators! And I was on *their* turf. Not a very good feeling.

Rosemarie Bowe, a woman I liked very much, was my co-star, and, later on, a terrible thing happened to her. The coral comes close to the surface of the ocean where we were. She was swimming back to shore, and she suddenly let out a horrible scream. Apparently, there is an animal that lives in crevices of that coral—I wish I knew what it was called—and it's covered with barbed spines like a porcupine. Rosemarie's arm had gotten too close to that creature. She couldn't see him, of course, and he'd whacked her and left hundreds of spines in her poor arm. I yelled for one of the men in a boat, a guy who steers it with one oar, to go help her. They got her into a boat with the cameras and crew—and her arm, oh God, it was terrible to see. At least the barbs weren't poisonous, but she was in horrible, terrible pain. I felt so, so awful for her, that nice woman. I really don't know what they did, but obviously they got her to a hospital, and I can only hope she was put to sleep before they cut those terrible things out of her arm. Rosemarie later married Robert Stack.

The movie was a good omen for me, however, because after it came out, Universal-International saw it and put me under contract. The first movie they put me in was *Revenge of the Creature*. It was 1954, and that's when my sci-fi film career began. I did a Western called *Star in the Dust*, and that was the only thing I did for Universal that wasn't sci-fi. When my contract came up for renewal in 1957, I remember talking with a vice president, saying to him that it bothered me that Jeff Chandler, Tony Curtis and Rock Hudson were all under contract with Universal, and they were getting normal movies. I asked him if I, too, couldn't stop making the sci-fi films and get into regular films like those guys. He told me he could not give me any guarantees. It was then I made what was probably a stupid mistake, and said to him, "Well, no hard feelings, but I think I'll just go out on my own, if that's the case."

And so I did. But it worked out well, because AIP offered me *Daughter of Dr. Jekyll*, which, of course, was another sci-fi, but I did it, anyway. As I've said before, a guy's got to eat and support his family. I continued making movies in that genre, not all sci-fi (like *The Brain from Planet Arous*). I did some more Westerns, and then did cameo work, once with John Wayne down in Mexico, so I was able to eke out a living doing what I love to do more than anything else on earth—acting. I guess I'll have to admit that, back then, I felt maybe some shame doing those films, and I shouldn't have. But none of us can read the future, and how could I know those old sci-fi films would be so beloved so many years later? I read that they're rented all the time and that people love them, and people surely do want my autograph on photos taken from those great old films. So now, as I look back, I realize I was an important part of film history and that those crazy sci-fi films I made were the precursors of the remarkable special effects horror and sci-fi films made today. I am very proud now of my body of work, very proud, indeed.

But, sadly, as often as these films are shown on TV and even in theaters, I get no residuals from them. Residuals only began after 1960, and all those films were made before that time. It's a sad state of affairs; so many of us old-time movie folk would be living a much more secure life if we could get those checks, but we can't. I do, however, get a monthly pension from SAG (Screen Actors Guild) and have for many years now and, while it's not a gigantic amount of money, it lets me live in some comfort. And I do get my social security, of course.

Loretta and I were unable to have children. She was told that a pregnancy might kill her. It wasn't worth taking the chance, so we began to talk

LORETTA AND I SIX DAYS AFTER GETTING MARRIED.

With my son, M.D.

about adoption. In 1958, Loretta and I flew down to Ft. Worth, and we picked out a son for ourselves at the children's home Edna Gladney, my great-aunt, ran. We saw him and loved him—a brand-new baby boy, just a few days old, that we'd be able to bring into our family after the legalities of adopting from a different state were straightened out. We named him Martin David, and called him M.D., and he's been a great son.

We had to leave him there at first and go back to California, however, but when everything was straightened out, we went back to get M.D. and brought him home. The biological mother had terminated all her rights to ever get in touch with him throughout his whole life, and the only way they can ever meet is if M.D. wants to have that happen. Thus far, he hasn't told us that he wants to meet her. He seems to have never had much interest. Loretta and I would not have objected at all.

M.D. was six years old in 1964 when, one day, Loretta's sister called us. An attorney had called her about a baby that was being put up for adoption, and she wanted to know if we were interested in having him. At first, Loretta said no, she really was content with just one child, but she couldn't get the idea of that little baby boy out of her mind. Finally, she called her sister back and said, "I've been thinking about that baby and have changed my mind. Yes, we'd really like to adopt him." John George Agar III had been born in

With my son, M.D.

My grandson, Ryan

John Agar III, me, Loretta, and M.D in front of our Encino home in 1971.

M.D., myself, and Loretta at a surprise 70th birthday party

Ryan, M.D., granddaughter Misty, and the old man

My Granddaughter Misty's graduation and prom pictures

Glendale Hospital, not far from here, and at three days old was waiting for us to come take him home, which we did. We were a complete family now.

ME, M.D., LORETTA, AND JOHN III

John does know his birth mother. Her name is Judy; she lives in Southern California, and I know her, too. I know they're on the phone often, so I have to assume it's a friendly relationship. It's a pretty private affair between John and his biological mother, and I don't want to interfere. John actually found her in a strange way. (I guess it's not so strange by today's standards, but it was to me, being born when there were no such things as computers.) One of Loretta's nieces found out who John's biological mother was by searching the Internet, and she located her, and so we got to meet Judy and her husband. Judy was only 17 when John was born and, knowing she could not care for him, that brave young woman gave him up. We've always been grateful to her for that. Judy is a wonderful woman, really terrific, and we like her very much. John has also been a great son.

As everyone knows, B movies never really paid the actors very much money, and now that I had a wife and two sons to support, I had to think about doing something else to bring in some income, so I became involved in selling life insurance. But I didn't like that very much, I really didn't, and wasn't awfully good at convincing people to buy something they maybe didn't want.

And then one day M.D., working for a place that delivered frozen meat in trucks to fast food and regular restaurants, heard about an opening, so I applied, got the job and began to work there. I was driving a truck, delivering one-hundred-pound boxes of frozen meat. Ironic, isn't it? After all, I'd been born into the meat-packing business in 1921. I'm sure people think it was embarrassing to me when people recognized me while I was doing that job, but I can honestly say it was not. A man has to make a living, and it was an honorable way to do it. I wasn't robbing banks, after all. At least I was employed and making enough money to support my family, but I did yearn to get back into movies again, so when the opportunity to work in a film was offered to me, I grabbed at it.

Loretta and I were so glad to have our two sons, and they gave us great joy. Unfortunately, though, their educations weren't as fulfilled as we'd have liked. John left school in the ninth grade because he was just so bored with it. He was so bright and so way ahead of all the other kids that he couldn't see much point in staying. We wish he had, but had to respect his decision. M.D. graduated from high school and attended Texas A&M for a year, but then left. M.D. did get his A.A. in Business/Marketing from Los Angeles Valley College. He came back to live with Loretta and me in our Burbank home for a while and became involved with the Brunswick Bowling company, working up in Palmdale at the bowling center. When he was 23 years old, he got married. They had a daughter, Misty, went to Tennessee with Brunswick and, sadly, he got divorced. He married again, he had a son, Ryan, by this marriage, and then got involved in the courier business. Today, M.D. works hard for his family and is still involved in the courier business. He is a member of the Professional Bowlers' Association and bowls part time on the PBA tour locally in California. M.D. later married Patty, his present wife, and, as they say, the third one's the charm. She's a terrific gal! He really found the right one. She comes from a great family. They have a beautiful daughter named Madison, but let me state here that my other two grandchildren are every bit as wonderful and important to me as they were to Loretta. I am very blessed.

John today is very involved in the computer world and has many ideas and plans. Of course, I really don't have any idea what he's talking about because there were no such things when I was a kid. I hope he'll

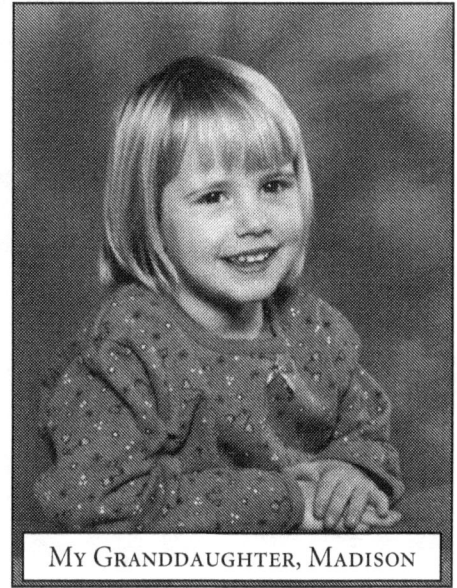

MY GRANDDAUGHTER, MADISON

have a big career in that field. He does love it. As of now, he's unmarried. I am very, very proud of my two sons. They were and are the lights of our lives.

I really enjoy going to huge autograph shows, or paper shows. These are held a couple of times a year, usually at big hotels. Movie stars, mostly older ones, all arrive at a huge hotel, where rows and rows of card tables are set up all around an enormous ballroom or conference room. Each table is assigned to a star, where we sit with stacks of photos of ourselves from when we were younger, often stills from the movies we were best remembered in. I go to these occasions whenever I can, and I have before me several large stacks of photos of me in my Western movies and sci-fi films, and I am proud to say that I get a great number of people coming up to my table to talk with me, to

WITH LORETTA AT AN AUTOGRAPH SHOW

tell me what they thought of my films and to buy the pictures. I don't charge as much as the other stars do at those autograph shows. I'm not trying to sound like a goody-goody, but I just can't do it. Maybe I'm weird, but I keep the prices of my 8x10s lower than others as my way of saying "thank you" to the public who have gone to see my movies. I'm genuine about this; I really am grateful that they went and that they've been in touch with me over the years and have remained loyal to me. I am grateful.

LOVE DOING THOSE AUTOGRAPH SHOWS!

Do I still get recognized? Amazingly, I do. I mean, people don't run after me in the street, but every so often they really do recognize me and come up and say hello and ask me if I'm "really John Agar." I've never had plastic or cosmetic surgery and never will, and my age definitely shows. This movie business can be such a harsh way to make a living, you know, very cruel. One never knows if one is going to have an income or if it's all going to last or not.

You know, basically, I have to do what I feel is right. As I've mentioned before in this book, my parents really did a good job raising us, and they gave us a strong sense of ethics and proper behavior, so I've never really gotten into the sort of Hollywood "cutthroat" mentality. I've had to do the right thing whenever I could and whenever I should. I can't say I haven't failed, because, of course, I have. I'm human and I'm flawed, but I've never been able to be part of a group or a scene where people trashed one another and stepped on each other to get ahead. Who knows? Maybe I could have been a huge star if I had, but I have to look into the mirror every morning, and I have to face my own conscience and my own God, and so I am what I am, as Popeye says. I have to do what I do in my own way and, in the main, I feel good about myself. I've tried to be a good person and lead a good life. I just can't see the point of stepping on anyone for doing what they do or for how they do it, if that's their choice. And don't forget, cosmic law or casting your bread upon waters, or whatever goes around comes around—whatever you want to call it—if you damage another person by word or deed, it will come back to you. It definitely will. I know it, I believe it, and it is the credo I live by.

JUNE WILKINSON and JOHN AGAR
in
PAJAMA TOPS

Movies were beginning to dry up for me, although I was finding acting jobs here and there, some on TV. Around this time, I got into real estate, got my license and got quite involved in that. A friend of Loretta's had a husband who owned a lot of property up past the Palmdale area, and I did very well selling that property. I found I could sell well to people. But, alas, I did something really stupid again—I seem to be able to find ways to sabotage myself a lot—I took a drink again. A lot of drinks, unfortunately, and got myself fired. I cannot put the blame on anyone but myself. Loretta wasn't exactly pleased about it, but she was such a great lady and was so good to me even all through my mistakes. I was very, very fortunate to have had her in my life. She was an endless joy to me.

WITH LORETTA AT MY SURPRISE 70TH BIRTHDAY PARTY

And so it was that my pension began from SAG and my Social Security began in 1965, and I became more settled, I guess, and didn't struggle to find acting jobs, hoping, of course, that some would come to me, but not actively searching them out. Well, things were slowing down for me. I was getting the occasional acting job, but not too many. I guess my story is typical of many old film stars: lots of work and then dwindle time. They were just small parts. I just loved working, though. I still love acting more than anything else. Acting was another part of my life, walking onto a set and having lines thrown at you, the lights, the noise and the fun of it. I'd act every single day of my life if I could, if they'd have me. I still get small cameo roles from time to time, and I'll act in anything. Even commercials, if they'd hire me! And plays, too—not Shakespeare, of course, but I did some stage plays back in the 1960s—*Pajama*

Tops, for example. June Wilkenson was in that with me, and she has her own fan club, just as I have. She lives in Van Nuys. We traveled to different places in the country to do that play. Loretta came with us.

Doing plays is so very different from doing a movie. In a play, you begin at the beginning and go straight through it. In movies, you may film the final scene on the first day on the set. Sometimes in filmmaking it's very hard to keep everything in order in your head. You're saying goodbye to your leading lady on day one, and on day two you meet her for the first time, and on it goes. I sure think computers help keep all that in order these days. You have to keep asking yourself, "What brought me to this situation now?" in whatever scene you're playing, because you just have to get yourself "back into it" when it's been totally mixed up.

But in a play—oh, it's great. You get instant reaction to your lines, you go from A to Z, and it's more normal indeed than filmmaking. But even with all this, I discovered that stage plays weren't really all that appealing to me, although when I did live TV plays, they were enjoyable. I can't explain it, but it's how it is with me. And live TV is *really* scary. I did a war play on TV, live, and I remember that I was supposed to shoot a guy who came into our bunker and, to my horror, the gun didn't go off. I pulled the trigger. Nothing. So being the pro that I am, I thought, well, I've got a bayonet—I'll just stab the guy to death, which I did, aiming, of course, for the side of him so he wouldn't get hurt. And you can guess what happened. The soundman must not have been paying much attention because as I'm stabbing, BOOM! The gun, of course, goes off! I just kept on going.

But alas, I blew it again while I was working on *Pajama Tops* in St. Louis. I think sometimes I just don't know when I'm well off, or I have a need to destroy myself in some unconscious way. I will never know, but I made a major mistake. One night, and I have no idea why, I had a couple of drinks and went on stage drunk, and the director fired me on the spot. The understudy got my job. Loretta and I came on home, and she wasn't very pleased with me. One of the very wonderful things about my Loretta was that she always forgave me, loved me and stayed with me no matter what. How blessed I was to have had her as my wife.

Sometimes, I'm asked if I'd go into the movies today, and that's a hard question for me to answer. I'd learned to love acting so much and had a great deal of respect for the business back when I began, but I don't know. Today? This is difficult to answer. When I began acting, there was certainly violence in films, and sex, too, but the writers wrote the stories and the lines leaving everything up to the viewer's imagination. People had to think when they went to the movies back then. And everyone knows that things coming from one's imagination are far more intriguing and fascinating than having every-

WHEN I WAS WORKING FOR THE BRUNSWICK CORP. AS "SENIOR BOWLING ADVISOR."

everything just out there on the screen. The sexual goings-on are just too much today, and the profanity I find personally offensive. I could never curse and be profane like that in a film—I just simply could not do it. And I was never expected or asked to. I'll give you a great example: remember the movie, *The Quiet Man*, with John Wayne and Maureen O'Hara? Was there ever a movie more sexy than that? It was obvious and strong, yet we never saw anything happen between them, but we knew what was going on. That film let people use their imaginations.

And speaking of Maureen O'Hara, I can't say enough about that lady. What a fabulous woman she is. I only got to act with her in one film, *Big Jake*, where I played the foreman on her ranch. I got myself shot in that film, and I went sailing through the door. I wasn't "wired up" as they do sometimes, so that the actor can be jerked backwards by the wire at the instant the shot goes off. To the viewer, this looks as if the person who's been shot has been knocked backwards by the violence of the blast. Nope, I did that stunt myself and made my body shoot violently backward through that door.

Things today are so different in the movie business. There seems to be a lot more independent producers, and people aren't under contract as they used to be. The actors don't have that protection any longer. And if they think you're not going to make any money for them, then you're gone. Some of the old actors have been "allowed" to age. Look at Katharine Hepburn; she aged in front of all of us and kept on acting, and she still is, although at this point I think she's well into her nineties. Henry Fonda was allowed to age

AGAIN WITH THE LOVELY LORETTA

and stay in films, and he was never not great. He won the Academy Award for *On Golden Pond* when he was in his seventies.

And I'm strongly against all that awful violence. I know people complained back when I was making Westerns and the sci-fi films, saying that there was too much violence in them, too and, for the times, maybe there was. But, oh, how tame it all was compared to what's going on today. We hardly even showed blood when a guy got shot. But this long, drawn-out, horrible, gory, bloody stuff is sickening. It's gotten, I think, to where people expect it and won't go to a film unless it's in there. What a shame. Filmmakers are stuck with having to invent new and more terrible scenes of violence. I think seeing all that stuff really makes people not concerned when they see real-life violence right in front of them.

My health today isn't as good as I'd like it to be, and it's not all that easy for me to get to various locations to work, so that's a problem. I'll always have to have someone take me and get me back home. And furthermore, I'm picky. I just won't work for the sake of working. I mean, it would have to be a project I believe in. I refuse to use profanity or foul language in any way. Any film I appear in has to have integrity and honesty; without those things, I won't appear, no matter how much money is involved.

I'd like to say somethng to my readers, if I may. If I could, I'd like to try to convince any of you reading this book to please think about giving up smoking. Forgive my saying this, I don't mean to sound preachy, but I'm having a terrible time breathing today because I smoked so much. I began at twelve, did it in alleys with pals, and we smoked our heads off. That's what a "real man" did, after all, and we wanted desperately to be all grown up and to be "real men." I smoked for 45 years, and even though I quit over twenty years ago it was just too late. My parents both smoked, so I was used to it, although Mom quit after Kip was born. But that's no excuse for my keeping the habit going for so, so many years. I'm in serious trouble today because of my smoking. I'd give almost anything to convince you to stop smoking, or to at least never start. End of lecture!

She left me abruptly, Loretta did. We were planning to go somewhere and she said she wanted to go to her dressing table to put on her make-up. I waited and waited, and then went in to see what was keeping her. Loretta was slumped to one side, and at first I thought she'd fallen asleep. But when I touched her, I knew. Loretta had quite suddenly died. We called the paramedics, but they couldn't help her. It was awful. To suddenly be without my dearest love and dearest friend was more, I thought, than I could bear. But because I try to look at the brighter side of things, I think to myself that at least she wasn't faced with a long and lingering death. It was sudden and painless, a blood clot that she may have had all her life. I'll never know. I miss her terribly. She was my life. Would I ever get involved with another woman now that my Loretta is gone? No possible way! Loretta is still with me and will be forever. I have no wish to ever marry again. We would have been married for 49 years.

We were a churchgoing family when I was young, but when I got older I stopped going. After I grew up and married for the second time, my wife Loretta and I became members of the Christian Science Church, then later

AT VETERAN MEMORIAL CEMETERY IN WEST LOS ANGELES IN 2000

on we became members of The Infinite Way. Not too many people know about this. The man who started it was Joel Goldsmith, who was a Christian Scientist at one time, but began this new religion, or maybe it's better called a new way of thinking, in the forties or fifties. He made many tapes and gave classes all over the world. Loretta and I liked what we heard, and we became Joel's followers. The Infinite Way, which could be called "a within-ness," is still in existence, and many people are still very much involved in it. People still give lectures on the study, although we don't gather together in a church. It's a very spiritual program, and I listen to tapes every day and love, appreciate and gain great insight from the words that Joel speaks. This all helps me very much in my life, and has been especially helpful to me since my darling Loretta died.

I'm going to do something perhaps a little unorthodox here. Because I began writing this book maybe later than I should, my health was such that I was unable to spend as much time as I would have liked with my co-author, L.C. Van Savage, when she came to my home for the interviews. My emphysema surely didn't help, and I fear I left many things out.

My good friend, Mr. Ed G. Lousararian, the owner and Editor-in-Chief of that great magazine, *Wildest Westerns,* a magazine devoted to "the men and women who made wonderful contributions to western films, shows and music," has very kindly given me permission to reproduce here, word-for-word, an article he wrote in his premier collector's issue about me called *John Agar: Going the Extra Mile.* For me, it is the definitive John Agar article, written with kindness, respect and in perfect detail.

I fear when you read this much will be repetitious, but I want to reproduce it verbatim because Ed Lousararian got so many details into his article about me I had forgotten to speak about. And so, again, with Ed's kind permission, here are the words he wrote about me in 1998.

REVENGE OF THE CREATURE (1955)

Tarantula (1955)

THE MOLE PEOPLE (1956)

The Mole People (1956)

THE DAUGHTER OF DR. JEKYLL (1957)

ATTACK OF THE PUPPET PEOPLE (1958)

Attack of the Puppet People (1958)

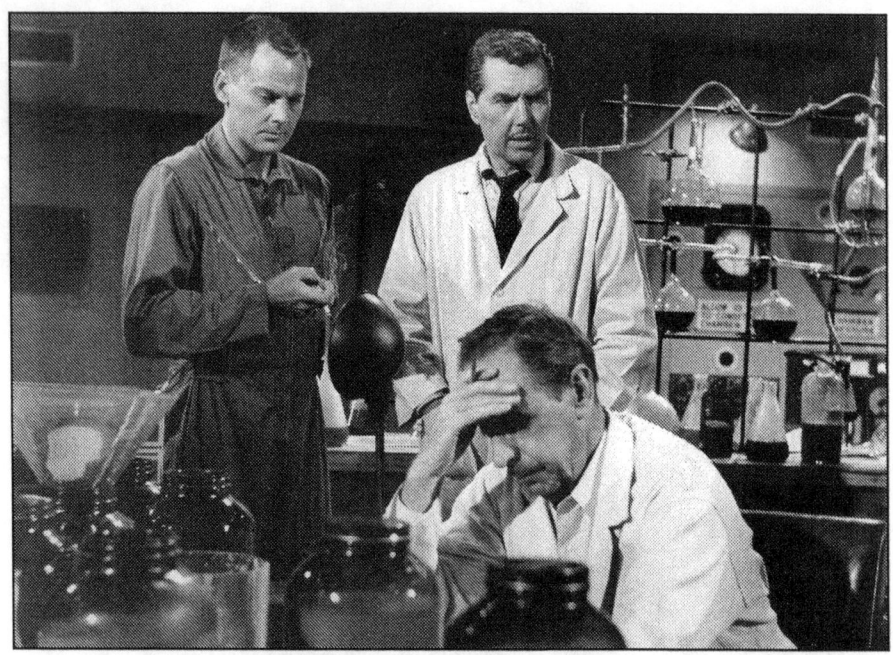

Invisible Invaders (1959)

The Young and the Brave (1963)

John Agar: Going The Extra Mile

Determined to confront the most important challenge in his acting career, John Agar made his debut in the big budget western, *Fort Apache*. The film's renowned director, John Ford, demanded nothing short of perfection, in spite of the fact that the rookie actor would have to support Hollywood heavyweights, John Wayne and Henry Fonda, who had 40 years of acting experience between them. Fortunately, perfection was Agar's aim, as he epitomized the valiant soldier and gallant gentleman Ford had envisioned him to project so poetically.

Ford, pleased with both Agar's outstanding performance and the commercial success of *Fort Apache* in 1948, awarded Agar the role of the bickering "Lieutenant Cohill" in *She Wore a Yellow Ribbon*. Ford knew he could bank on Agar's athletic abilities and positive mental attitude. With these two attributes, Ford had no trouble getting Agar to do anything the script warranted—even to ride a horse through a herd of buffalo!

THE GOLDEN BOOT AWARD

Consistently in the Top 25 most rented westerns, *Fort Apache* and *She Wore a Yellow Ribbon* are considered classics. Together with *The Searchers*, they comprise the famous "Cavalry Trilogy," which contributed to the reputation and respect Ford has earned as one of the greatest directors in motion picture history. Undeniably, Ford has left a legacy of greatness, of which John Agar is a part.

In a career embodying nearly 50 years of movie making, John Agar remains one of America's favorite cowboys, with 17 westerns to his credit. Additionally, Agar has been regarded as one of the true legends of the cult movie world.

An honored recipient of the Golden Boot Award, the Silver Boot Award, the Count Dracula Society Award, and the Science-Fiction Academy Award, Agar proved that he had established himself as one of the hardest working actors in Hollywood, always going the "extra mile" for the camera, no matter what project.

With a philosophy that each and every person working in front of or behind the camera has equally important roles, Agar's unselfish and caring work ethic translated both on and off screen. Even for pictures that Agar at times felt were a bit absurd, the dedicated actor made himself believe in each venture, and was willing to perform dangerous stunts to make a scene more realistic in his pursuit to make each film a success.

For example, not many actors would be willing to continue filming scenes while suffering with paint chips embedded in their eyes. Not many actors would be willing to be submerged in a tank and surrounded by sharks. Not many actors would be willing to stunt fall from a horse, or to suffocate in fat suits and rubber head masks, or to dive 40 feet below the ocean's surface on an aqualung with the threat of being struck with an air embolism. John Agar would, and did.

Agar was born in 1921 in the "Windy City," where he grew up with his younger siblings, sister Joyce and brothers Jim and Frank. The early years were happy times, but in 1935 at 14, he lost his father to a heart attack. John remembers, "My dad's passing was tough on us kids, but it was extremely tough on my mom. She was widowed with four hungry mouths to feed."

As times became more difficult for the Agars, so would they for America. World War II was on, and John, with patriotism in his blood, enlisted in the Army Air Corps, where he would serve as a physical training instructor and sergeant, commissioned to transform American recruits from greenhorns into fighting machines.

The first time Sgt. Agar appeared before the public eye was when he wed America's sweetheart, Shirley Temple, in 1945, but, thankfully, this would not be the public's last time to see him. Shortly thereafter, on a furlough, Sgt. Agar bumped into a gentleman at a party who asked the handsome young man what his post-service plans entailed. This gentleman was none other than the successful independent producer, David O. Selznick. John recalls, "I really hadn't given any thought as to what I was going to do when I'd get out. When Selznick asked if I had ever thought of being an actor, I laughed and told him that I was a meat packer's son from Chicago—

WHEN I WAS YOUNG...

that the thought of becoming an actor had never entered my mind. Selznick went on to tell me that he would like to test me to see if I had any acting ability and if so, he'd sign me and teach me." Agar took Selznick's words lightly, went back to his base, and two weeks later a surprise arrived in the mail. It was a test contract!

As World War II came to a close, Agar's mission to go overseas to bulldoze the aftermath of the atomic bombs in Hiroshima and Nagasaki was canceled, and most of the men were able to return home...but not Agar. The Army Air Corps, with its high demand for quality commanding officers, shipped him to Salt Lake City for four more months before he could return home.

Coming home from the war in 1946 and in desperate need of a job, Agar took Selznick up on his offer, walked onto the studio lot for his first screen test, and acted out a scene from *The Farmer's Daughter*. John recalls, "Selznick liked it and signed me and I don't have any idea why [laughs] because I got to see my screen test afterward and I thought it was terrible! So for one year I attended acting groups and studied diction." It was then that Agar was promoted to a salary of $150 a week, in sharp contrast to the $83 he earned in an entire month in the service.

Then, one day, serendipity struck again, when Agar's mother and sister took a cruise to Hawaii. John Ford (along with his wife, Mary, and daughter, Barbara) was on the cruise also, so when Agar went to pick up his family as the *Princess Cruise* docked at San Pedro, the Agars and the Fords became acquainted. The Agar family left quite an impression, because one week later, Selznick, who was on the same lot as Ford, approached Agar and said, "Go see Mr. Ford and Mr. [Merian C.] Cooper. They're going to be doing a movie and they want to see you."

John tells the story: "Ford had me standing at attention and doing right face and left, about face, and he asked, 'Were you in the service?' And I said, 'Yes sir.' He asked 'What branch?' And I said, 'Army Air Corps.' 'Oh,' Ford says, 'off we go into the wild blue yonder, crash!' And I said, 'Yeah. I guess you're right, sir. Were you in the service?' Ford said, 'Yeah, I was a commander in the United States Navy,' and I said, 'Oh, you mean anchors aweigh, sink, huh?' From then on it was smooth sailing, so to speak. Not many actors who crossed paths with John Ford, a man notorious for being strong-willed and fiery-tempered, had an easy time building rapport and reaching an understanding with him, yet Agar did. History was written, and John Agar had "broken" into the business. He secured his first acting role in *Fort Apache*, that masterful and initial film of Ford's "Cavalry Trilogy," and never looked back.

Agar, looking "at home" in westerns, especially with his professional gun handling and horsemanship, had an early start. When he was 11, he learned about ranching at a summer camp in Colorado. "I groomed my own horse, fed it...everyone was responsible for their own horses," says John. As an adult, Agar learned a lot more about horses the hard way, when he asked Jack Pennick (also in *Fort Apache*) to teach him riding tricks.

"Jack and I were riding all day," John recollects, "and boy, I was saddle-sore. When I got home to shower that evening, my rear was raw and bleeding. The next day on the set, I told Pennick what had happened, and he said, 'Oh, don't worry. Go to the drugstore and get some sea salt and pour it in the tub and then get in there and soak.' Well, I followed his medical advice, and when that salt hit my raw butt [laughs]...my screams could be heard around the world. And Pennick told everybody on the set about that. He really made me look like an idiot."

It didn't take long however, for this rising young star to make friends in Hollywood. "I can't say enough about Duke Wayne, John Ford, [Victor] McLaglen, and [Ward] Bond," remarks Agar. "They took the big brother approach and were always there to advise and encourage me."

Off the set, Agar's friendly, outgoing nature, coupled with his strong passion for the sport of golf, prompted his membership in the Hollywood Hackers, where he would swing mean clubs with fellow actors Richard Arlen, Alan Hale, Jr., James Gregory and Claude Akins.

In 1950, Agar's marriage to Shirley Temple fell apart and they decided to call it quits. Later that year, he met a beautiful dancer named Loretta at the Riviera Country Club through mutual friends of theirs. Loretta had worked a sister act in a score of Betty Grable and Alice Faye movies, as well as appearing in Orson Welles' monumental *Citizen Kane*. She appeared later in Jack Arnold's thriller, *Revenge of the Creature*, also with John. On May 16, 1951, John and Loretta were married and they stayed together until her death in 1999.

It was also in 1951 that David O. Selznick went out of business, leaving his last male contract player to do freelance acting for the next three years. Agar worked on numerous films during that period, including Raoul Walsh's masterpiece, *Along the Great Divide*. In this Western, Agar's character, as the deputy protecting Walter Brennan from a lynch mob, is martyred; his dying scene is moving and all the more convincing because Agar insisted that no stunt double be used. Just as James Stewart, at his own suggestion, was dragged through a campground fire in *The Man from Laramie*, it was Agar in *Along the Great Divide* who leaped from his horse, taking a nose-dive onto the hot sand of the Mojave Desert.

Another film—a rarely-seen, cult classic—*The Golden Mistress* with Rosemarie Bowe, deserves attention for two reasons. First, when filming on location in the Caribbean, Agar encountered unsavory situations triggered by the gutsy stunts required for the script. Upon reflection, Agar said that he would probably never do "some of those things" today with what he knows now.

"We filmed a scene on a lake between the Dominican Republic and Haiti," John reports, "and we're in this murky water all day long. As we're packing up for the day, I look around and I see something moving around, and I'm wondering what the heck it is. Then to my amazement it started to surface…alligators….a dozen of them. We had been swimming with alligators all day long and didn't even know it. That was quite a film—I did a dive 60 feet high from the top of a mast and [laughs] they never even used the footage."

Secondly, when this film was seen by the powers that be at Universal, Agar's performance and screen presence so impressed them that he was signed to a contract in 1954.

Agar's debut film with his new studio was a lead role in William Alland and Jack Arnold's ever-popular thriller, *Revenge of the Creature*. For the next two years he worked rigorously, never refusing to do a film or a stunt that he was asked to do.

However, when Agar's contract came up for renewal, he was disturbed, and with good reason. This was a time when Universal was pushing Rock Hudson, Tony Curtis and Jeff Chandler for stardom. They were given the serious, dramatic roles, yet whenever a science-fiction project came along, the producers sought out John Agar. As a matter of fact, Rock Hudson paid a visit to Agar one day on the set of *The Mole People*, when Hudson, in a condescending manner posed the question, "How did you get mixed up in this thing?"

Enough was enough! Agar stormed through the office of the Vice President at Universal (Jim Pratt) saying, "Look, I'd just like to have the same kind of shot as the rest of these guys instead of doing solely science-fiction." The response was not what he expected: "Well, we can't make any guarantees." With that utterance, John wished him the best and went out to freelance. Today John laughs about it. He says, "So I go out and freelance and go right back into science fiction again." Agar continued to work steadily in a slew of films, and later teamed up with A. C. Lyles at Paramount to headline westerns with the likes of Dana Andrews, Jane Russell, Dale Robertson, Yvonne De Carlo, and Rory Calhoun. Notwithstanding, toward the late 1970s Agar became disenchanted with the movie industry and began to shift his efforts to the business world, where he also has achieved success.

With a film career spanning nearly five decades and a myriad of fans from three different genres—western, science fiction and horror—John Agar has become a Hollywood icon. In a fourth genre—a war film—Agar once again rises to the occasion in the critically acclaimed *Sands of Iwo Jima*. It's surprising that he didn't pick up an Oscar for his immaculate and meticulous performance as the bitter, hardheaded, intellectual marine—one of the few cinematic characters to ever get the last word in with John Wayne.

In addition to starring roles with Wayne and Fonda, Agar has worked with top performers such as Clint Eastwood, Lucille Ball, Kirk Douglas, Maureen O'Hara and Michael Landon.

Today, since the death of his beloved Loretta, John resides in Burbank, California. They have two adopted sons, Martin (M.D.) and John III.

In the celebrated life of this talented and daring man, it's no wonder that an amusement park is named after him ("Agar's Land of Kong"), and that thousands of fans flock to see him at collectors' shows throughout the country. John Agar's popularity is a testament to the kindness of the man and the versatility of the "Extra Mile Actor."

AGAR ON WESTERNS

I enjoy westerns immensely. I would've liked to have done more TV westerns, though. I did a *Bat Masterson*—Gene Barry helps me out in a gun showdown. And I was up for an episode of *Have Gun Will Travel*, but for some reason my agent turned it down. I enjoyed working on *Rawhide*, *Death Valley Days*, *The Virginian*, *Branded* and *Hondo*.

AGAR ON JOHN FORD

We hit it off. It's funny—Wayne, Fonda, George O'Brien—they'd tell me that after knowing Ford for years, they couldn't tell when he was kidding, when he was serious, and that I best be careful. I always considered Ford a kidder, so I'd just kid him right back.

Anything Ford did was great. He was the best director ever, especially considering how long he was making movies. The man was brilliant.

AGAR ON JOHN WAYNE

He was in the top ten for over 40 years…I was lucky to work with him. I'll tell you, Duke was a neat guy. The best.

We did five films together. When we did *She Wore a Yellow Ribbon*, I thought Duke's performance was worthy of an Oscar nomination, and they gave him nothing. They nominated him for *Sands of Iwo Jima*, and still nothing. And then it took 20 years before he ever won anything—for *True Grit*. Twenty years! Ridiculous!

AGAR ON HOLLYWOOD

For many films today, the substance isn't there. Instead, you get sex, violence, and special effects. And what about character actors? Do you remember Frank McHugh and that funny laugh of his? And Allen Jenkins, Edgar Buchanan, Bing Russell, Dub Taylor, Don Collier, Hugh Beaumont...? Those guys were super. We don't have people like them anymore.

AGAR ON CO-STARS

Richard Boone: I knocked him off in *Star in the Dust*, but he got even with me [laughs] when he blew me away in *Big Jake*. He was serious on screen, but behind the scenes, he was a funny fellow. We got along fine.

Lon Chaney Jr.: We worked together in a couple of westerns. He was a nice guy. I think he drank himself to death. Too bad. I always liked him.

Kirk Douglas: I worked with him in his first western—*Along the Great Divide*. Kirk and I never got that close to each other. I never quite understood him. I didn't dislike him. He and I have completely different outlooks on life, that's all.

Maureen O'Hara: The first time I met her was when we were working together in *Big Jake*, and I couldn't believe how gorgeous she was. At that time, she was in her early 50s, and I thought, "Wow, she looks like she's in her 30s!" She's a fantastic lady! A joy to work with.

Michael Landon: I was up for an episode of *Highway to Heaven*, and I met with Michael Landon to read for him. So Michael signed me. He said, "You're the guy I want." So...it was a lot of fun, I really enjoyed it. Michael told me he was very happy with my work [laughs] but I never worked for him again. Nice man. It was so sad to see him pass on, especially at such an early age. He could write, produce, direct, act...that's incredible. He was an incredible guy.

AGAR ON SHIRLEY TEMPLE

I have no ill feelings. I just think we were both too young. The only thing that has been kind of rough over the years is that we have a daughter, Susan, and I haven't seen her since she was six years old. I did get a chance to talk to her on the phone, but...she has changed her telephone number. I wasn't trying to push myself into her life. I just thought that we could be acquainted, and if she didn't want to be around me, there wouldn't be any hard feelings. But I can understand her situation because I think if we did start becoming friends, Susan would probably feel she'd be letting her mother down, and I can understand that.

AGAR ON ACTING

I look at acting as a job, and all this hype and glorification to me is just bunk. It's...you show up on time, you know your lines, do your job, and...Duke taught me that. John Wayne, Henry Fonda, Jimmy Stewart, Gregory Peck, Gary Cooper—they were marvelous. They could do more with a look or expression that could tell you exactly what's going on in the scene. Very important for me are the subtleties of acting, which in that day in time were tremendous.

AGAR ON CLINT EASTWOOD

I called Clint at Warner Brothers after he won his two Oscars (for *Unforgiven*)...I left a couple of messages...and finally I thought, "Well, OK, I guess we're not going to connect." Then one night Clint called back, and I told him how happy I was for him, and he was pleased. We were both under contract at Universal, and his first movie was *Revenge of the Creature*, where he played a lab assistant and he had [laughs] that mouse in his pocket. In Clint's second film [*Tarantula*, also with Agar], he played the jet pilot who dropped the napalm on the tarantula...and he was in a western I did called *Star in the Dust*...with Richard Boone and Mamie Van Doren. Clint's a great guy.

AGAR ON ODDITIES

Oddity one: In *Johnny Reno*, the Indians think I'm the bad guy who mistreated them, so they torture me. Then, as they were dragging me into town on a travois, something spooked the horse, and he kicked the heck out of everything in his path. He just missed my head! So the director said, "We're not gonna bring you in like that. The Indians are gonna bring you in on the horse." So as we're going through the scene, we come riding in and the read bad guy in town gets cued—he pulls his gun. Um, they forgot to rehearse this with the horse [laughs]. BOOM! I'm shot...the horse reared with the shot, and I flew clear over his back and landed right in horse dung. It was fresh too—he had just done it, and I fell right in the middle of it.

Oddity two: One thing I've always been very curious about. I have never found out why. It was 20 years after shooting *Sands of Iwo Jima* that I worked with Duke Wayne again in *The Undefeated*. Duke and I had a very emotional scene together on horseback which shows the loyalty of all the guys who were on the horse drive with him. A number of us in the story had gotten ill, and I tell Duke, "I can't go on." He says, "Well, when we sell the horses, I'll send your cut to your family," because he knows I'm going to die. And they cut that whole doggone scene out. I have not seen that scene to this day, but Lee Meriwether [who also worked in *The Undefeated*] saw it and said she didn't understand why it was cut—she thought it was a great scene. If you watch the film, you'll notice that Duke mentions having "a friend who won't make Christmas," but the way the film is edited, how's the audience supposed to know who or what he's talking about?

Oddity three: Twenty years ago, I went downtown to a science-fiction convention at the Biltmore, and Loretta and I walked in, and a young guy walks up to me and says, "Hey, you're John Agar." I said "Yeah." He says, "Stay right there." Pretty soon this guy comes back and says, "It is you!" I said, "What?" This guy thought I was dead. Later Forry Ackerman walks up and tells me, "Oh John, I just wrote your obituary." I said, "Really? I may be dead, but I haven't got the sense enough to lie down." Turns out he heard from the Academy that I had passed on, and he printed my obituary in his magazine, *Famous Monsters of Filmland*.

FORRY ACKERMAN AND J.A.

It's time to end this book now. I hope I haven't come across as too self-serving. My parents taught us kids to have integrity, to behave in responsible and honest ways, to be polite and good, kind when we could and to never downgrade another human being. I've tried to keep up with this code. It is how I wish to honor them. It is how I wish to honor my life and my family. I have made many mistakes. I take full responsibility for them all. I think I can truly say I've done my best and, although it hasn't always worked out for the best, I've tried hard. Today, I live in an assisted-living place in Burbank, and I'm happy here. I miss Loretta very much, but I can have family near to me when I need them, John III and M.D. I have a steady stream of friends who invite me everywhere and come by to visit. I think I am liked by them. They matter to me, and they've helped me through the hard times. Do I have regrets? Sure I do. I could never say, "I wouldn't change one minute of my life." I can't understand people who say that. It's impossible to not have regrets. I just won't dwell on those things. My life is coming to an end, and I look back on it all and smile. I have been awfully lucky in a lot of ways. I thank you for reading my story. God Bless.

Filmography

FEATURE FILMS:

- 1948: Fort Apache (2nd Lt. Michael Shannon O'Rourke)
- 1949: Adventure in Baltimore (Tom Wade)
  I Married a Communist (Don Lowry)
  She Wore a Yellow Ribbon (Pfc. Peter Conway)
- 1950: Breakthrough (Lt. Joe Mallory)
- 1951: Along the Great Divide (Billy Shear)
  The Magic Carpet (Abdullah al Husan/Dr. Ramoth/The Scarlet Falcon)
- 1952: Woman of the North Country (David Powell)
- 1953: Man of Conflict (Ray Compton)
- 1954: Bait (Ray Brighton)
  The Rocket Man (Tom Baxter)
  Shield for Murder (Det. Sgt. Mark Brewster)
  The Golden Mistress (Bill Buchanan)
- 1955: Revenge of the Creature (Prof. Clete Ferguson)
  The Lonesome Trail (Johnny Rush)
  Hold Back Tomorrow (Joe Cardos)
  Tarantula (Dr. Matt Hastings)
- 1956: Star in the Dust (Sheriff Bill Jorden)
  The Mole People (Dr. Roger Bentley)
- 1957: Flesh and the Spur (Lucius "Luke" Random/Matt Random)
  Joe Butterfly (Sgt. Dick Mason)
  The Brain from Planet Arous (Steve March)
  Ride a Violent Mile (Jeff Dunning)
- 1958: Jet Attack (Capt. Tom Arnett)
  Attack of the Puppet People (Bob Westley)
  Frontier Gun (Sheriff Jim Crayle)
- 1959: Invisible Invaders (Maj, Bruce Jay)
- 1960: Raymie (Ike)
- 1961: Fall Girl (Joe McElroy)
- 1962: Journey to the Seventh Planet (Capt. Don Graham)
  Hand of Death (Alex Marsh)
- 1963: The Young and the Brave (Intelligence Captain)
  Of Love and Desire (Gus Cole)
  Cavalry Command (Sgt. Judd Norcutt)
- 1964: Law of the Lawless (Pete Stone)

	Stage to Thunder Rock (Dan Carrouthers)
1965:	Young Fury (Dawson)
1966:	Johnny Reno (Ed Tomkins)
	Women of the Prehistoric Planet (Dr. Farrell)
	Waco (George Gates)
1967:	Night Fright (Sheriff Clint Crawford)
	The St. Valentine's Day Massacre (Dion O'Bannion)
1969:	The Undefeated (Christian)
1970:	Chisum (Amos Patton)
1971:	How's Your Love Life? (Police Lt. Rafferty)
	Big Jake (Bert Ryan)
1976:	King Kong (City Official)
1981:	Mr. No Legs (Police Captain)
1982:	Divided We Fall (Yankee Officer)
1988:	Perfect Victims (Neighbor)
	Miracle Mile (Ivan Peters)
1989:	Stepgather II (Cameo)
1990:	Nightbreed (Special Appearance)
	Fear (Leonard Scott Levy)
2005:	The Naked Monster (Dr. Clete Ferguson) (filmed in 1995)

TELEVISION MOVIES:

1959:	Destination Space (Col. Matthews)
1966:	Zontar, the Thing from Venus (Dr. Curt Taylor)
	Curse of the Swamp Creature (Barry Rogers)
1968:	Hell Raiders (Maj. Ronald Paxton)
1991:	The Perfect Bride (Gramps)
1992:	Invasion of Privacy (Old Convict)
1993:	John Carpenter Presents Body Bags: Eye (Dr. Lang)

TELEVISION GUEST APPEARANCES:

1952:	Hollywood Opening Night ("Delaying Action")
	Fireside Theater ("The Next to Crash")
	The Unexpected ("Desert Honeymoon")
1953:	Ford Television Theater ("Old Man's Bride")
	Letter to Loretta ("Earthquake")
1954:	Schlitz Playhouse of Stars ("Little War at San Dede")
	Fireside Theater ("The Farnsworth Case")
	G.E. Theater ("Desert Crossing")

1955: Climax! ("The First and the Last")
1957: G.E. Theater ("Thousand Dollar Gun")
1958: The Gale Storm Show ("Diamonds are a Girl's Best Friend")
Whirlybirds ("Four Little Indians")
1959: Perry Mason ("The Case of the Caretaker's Cat")
Rawhide ("Incident at the Buffalo Smokehouse")
1960: Rawhide ("Incident of the Slavemaster")
1961: Ripcord ("Chuting Stars")
The Best of the Post ("Band of Brothers")
Bat Masterson ("Farmer with a Badge")
1962: Lawman ("The Witness")
Here's Hollywood
1963: Death Valley Days ("Pioneer Doctor")
1964: The Virginian ("Walk in Another's Footsteps")
1965: Branded ("$10,000 for Durango")
1966: Combat! ("The Mockingbird")
1967: Family Affair ("What Did You Do in the West, Uncle?")
Hondo ("Hondo and the Judas")
1968: The Name of the Game ("Nightmare")
The Virginian ("The Mustangers")
1974: Chase ("Remote Control")
1976: Police Story ("The Long Bull")
1976: Charlie's Angels ("Target: Angels")
1984: Highway to Heaven ("Return of the Masked Rider")
1986: The Twilight Zone ("A Day in Beaumont")

Misc. Credits:

1961: Fall Girl (sings title song)
1996: The Pandora Directive (voice only; video game) (Thomas Malloy)
2001: The Vampire Hunters Club (straight-to-video) (Reggie)

Appendix

Two interviews with John Agar
by Tom Weaver

In certain circles, Jack Arnold is considered one of science fiction's top talents. How did you enjoy working with him?

I've always had nothing but great respect for Jack Arnold. I did *Revenge of the Creature* for him and then the next year we did *Tarantula*, and we got along very well. So far as I was concerned, he was a very knowledgeable director and he gave his all trying to make 'em the best that he could. Jack is a great guy; I don't think Universal was too kind to Jack, I think he should have been given a lot more opportunities. I went over and saw him at Universal a few years ago; he was going to do a remake of *The Lost World*, then all of a sudden the powers that be canceled the thing on him. Of course you know that Jack lost a limb [to cancer]. The people behind *The Lost World* were going to go over to England and shoot it and Jack really wanted to direct it, but they didn't feel that he could physically do it. Then they changed their minds about doing the picture at all.

Did you enjoy the location trip to Florida for Revenge of the Creature?

I had never been to Marineland, and that was a lot of fun. We all got kind of carried away on that picture—we started having water gun fights and, gosh, it got to the point where one guy got up on top of a cottage with a bucket of water and poured it all over a bunch of people!

Lori Nelson told us that that was the most fun she'd ever had making a movie.

We just had a heck of a good time. My wife, Loretta, joined me down there, and as a matter of fact she had a little part in the picture. Remember the scene at the Lobster House when the Creature abducts Lori, and I dive off the pier after them? After that there's a shot of a guy and a girl in a boat; the girl's my wife, Loretta.

Did you have to learn to use an aqualung for underwater scenes in Revenge?

I learned to use an aqualung before that. Shortly before I did *Revenge of the Creature*, I went down to the Caribbean and did a picture called *The Golden Mistress* [1954], and I had to learn to use an aqualung for the underwater scenes in the picture. Nobody down there seemed to know anything about them so I just went into the swimming pool at the hotel we were staying at, and I leaned to utilize it. It's not all that difficult, but the one thing I didn't know about using an aqualung is that you can get an air embolism mighty easy—if you surface too quickly and you're holding the air in, you can be in a lot of trouble. I got into a ticklish situation: The underwater cameraman and I were swimming around this sunken ship, about forty feet down. There were some breaks in the deck and shafts of sunlight were shining down into the hold, and the cameraman thought it would be interesting to get a shot in there. So I swam in there, clear to the bow of the ship; I went to take a breath, to get air—and I couldn't get it! So I had to swim about twenty feet to the hole, just to get out of the ship, and then I had to swim forty feet up before I could surface. And in coming up I could feel the pressure on my body easing, releasing. Luckily, Somebody was watching over me, and I guess He showed me what to do. I had the sense not to hold my breath, to let it out, as I came up. I could have gotten into some real problems there.

Wasn't it dangerous swimming in the Marineland tank with all those sharks?

I was told by the people who ran Marineland that those sharks were really not dangerous; I had a tiger shark, an eight-footer, swim right over my head and it didn't pay any attention to me. I know Ricou Browning, who did the underwater work as the Creature, was being pestered more by the big sea turtles than by anything else—they'd come up and nip at him! But I did have one experience that could have been a little disastrous. There's one part of the main tank that had a kind of rock formation just below the surface. During the scene where the Creature escapes—grabs Johnny Bromfield, throws him in the water and kills him—I was standing at the far end of the tank. Why I did this I will never know [*laughs*], but I dove back into the tank at that point, not realizing how close to the surface of the water those rocks were. If I hadn't flattened my dive at the last second, I would've hit 'em flush. This is just speculation, but if I had hit there hard and maybe gotten a bloody nose or something, it might have been a different kind of story, according to what I've heard about sharks and the way they smell blood out in water.

What can you tell us about working with Ricou Browning?

Ricou was one of the most fascinating people insofar as his swimming was concerned—he had lung capacity that was just incredible. They would drop an oxygen hose into that tank and he would breathe through it; the oxygen was coming out of there with pressure and it would fill up the Gill-Man suit. So after he'd gotten the amount of oxygen he wanted, he then had to press the suit and get all the bubbles out. Then he would go and do the scene. I could stay underwater for over two minutes if I wasn't doing anything, but this guy was swimming and using a lot of energy. How he did that was just really amazing and marvelous to watch.

Richard Carlson, who starred in the original Creature from the Black Lagoon, *once admitted that the Gill-Man suit seemed so real that he got spooked shooting scenes in the studio tank.*

Well, when you see something that unusual, even though you know it's all make-believe, it is kind of a strange experience. If this were a real creature, what it could do to you wouldn't be pretty. So I can understand Richard Carlson saying that, especially in an underwater situation.

Would you agree that Tarantula *is your best science fiction film?*

Yeah, I guess that would be the one; [*laughs*] I really don't know. I am the worst judge of what I've done; I can see where I could have been so much better, could've done such a better job than what I did. I can always see that.

I had never planned to be an actor, and it was thrust upon me at a very early age. It was something I really wasn't ready for. Now I know exactly what George Bernard Shaw meant when he said that youth is wasted on the young.

William Alland, who produced Revenge, Tarantula *and other Jack Arnold films, once said that he feels slighted because Arnold seems to get all the credit for them nowadays. Was Alland a creative force as well?*

I agree wholeheartedly that William Alland was a force. He was the one that came up with some of the ideas and he produced the films, and he shouldn't be slighted at all. Those pictures, whether Universal wants to admit it or not, were moneymakers. There were three Creature pictures made, and I was told by a producer at Universal, Aaron Rosenberg, that *Revenge of the Creature* was the biggest grosser of all of 'em. I also heard that *Tarantula* was one of the top grossers of 1955; what they probably meant was that it was a top moneymaker in terms of what it cost and what it brought in, but I had heard that it was Number 5 in 1955.

The Mole People *is by far the least of your three sci-fi Universals. Would you put the blame on first-time director Virgil Vogel?*

Oh, no—Virgil Vogel is a nice guy and I don't blame that on Virg, heck, no. But to me, *The Mole People* was like some of those Larry Buchanan things I did down in Texas for money. In fact, it was right after *The Mole People* that I left Universal. I was there at the same time that they were grooming Tony Curtis, Rock Hudson, Jeff Chandler, George Nader—and I always kept getting the science fiction pictures. While I was under contract, the only Universal picture I did that wasn't sci-fi was a Western called *Star in the Dust* [1956]; that worked out well, and I felt that I didn't want to be just science fiction all the time. Bill Alland, for some reason, wanted me in all of his science fiction pictures, and when they came up with this one…well [*laughs*], the story just didn't gel with me at all. People coming up out of the ground looking like moles, and an underground civilization.

Too far out?
    Yeah. I remember, too, that there was some silly dialogue in *The Mole People*, and I went to Bill Alland and told him, "Bill, people don't say things like this." He said something to the effect that he paid a guy a lot of money to write that dialogue, and I said, "Well, you got cheated!" And I think my nose got out of joint one time when I was on the set and Rock Hudson came over. He looked around at the production that was going on and he said, "How'd you get into *this* thing?" It was the kind of derogatory way that he said it—I don't know whether he meant it or not, but [*laughs*] that frosted me a little bit. I just never thought that *The Mole People* was as good a picture as *Revenge of the Creature* or *Tarantula*.

As a Universal contract player, were you in a position to turn down an assignment?
    When you're under contract to a studio or to a producer and they assign you a project, if you don't do it they can put you on suspension and for the duration of that film you go without pay. I never turned anything down. They were paying me, and I figured that they were doing what was best for everybody concerned—not only for the studio but for me as well, because I was a member of their team, so to speak. Maybe I was naïve, but I trusted them to guide my career.

Did you feel that the mole monsters in The Mole People *were effective?*
    They were all right for the time; they didn't have the technology we have today. But at that time I thought that Universal had some of the best technicians in the business, as far as science fiction was concerned.

How was the special effect of men being dragged down under the earth achieved?
    They put a rubber mat down over a hole in the floor; the mat had an X-shaped slit in it. Then they covered it with some kind of light material—it could have been Styrofoam—that was supposed to be earth or gravel. Even when someone was being pulled down through from below, the earth was held up—a lot of it could not fall through at once. The remaining earth would then cover up where they went though.

Why did you leave Universal after The Mole People*?*
    I talked with Jim Pratt, who was the vice president over there, and I told him, "You know, I understand that you-all are grooming particular people,

but I just don't want to do all these science fiction pictures." So when my option time came up, I said that I'd just as soon not stay on, and I didn't. I don't know, maybe I made a mistake, maybe they might've turned around and given me other things to do. I've made a lot of mistakes in my life [*laughs*], and maybe that was one of 'em.

One of your first pictures after leaving Universal was Daughter of Dr. Jekyll. *Were you disappointed to still be in that sci-fi/horror rut?*
   Well—yeah. I really didn't want to do any more of those pictures, but [*laughs*] at least I made more money on *Daughter of Dr. Jekyll* than Universal was paying me!

What do you remember about your co-star, Gloria Talbott?
   I really thought she was going to go on to do better things, but then what I guess happened was that she got married and got smart, and got out of the business. She was a very nice gal and we tried to do the best we could with *Daughter of Dr. Jekyll*. Some of those things work and some of 'em don't.

Did Daughter of Dr. Jekyll *work?*
   Not really. I did that picture strictly for the bread. I didn't fluff it—I did the best I could with what I had to work with—but it wasn't my cup of tea. I just didn't believe it.

When you weren't appearing in a science fiction film, it was usually a Western or a war picture. Were you more comfortable in those genres?
   To me, it's a lot easier to play in something that's real—a natural situation—than it is to deal with abstracts and things of the unknown. It's sort of difficult to make them come to life [*laughs*]! I always kind of had the feeling that when people looked at some of these science fiction things, we were going to get a big laugh. On a couple of occasions, some of the things that were supposed to frighten people really looked rather ludicrous—funny, rather than scary. I feel it's more natural to deal in something that people understand, rather than something that human beings don't come in contact with. It's a touchy situation to be in.

Did you enjoy playing a villainous Jekyll and Hyde-style role in The Brain from Planet Arous?
   Yes, and I wish I had gotten more opportunities to play against type. I'll tell you one thing, that picture was a very painful experience for me. When that alien being took over my body, they inserted these full contact lenses in my eyes. They'd painted 'em silver and they forgot that that doggone paint

would chip off. Every time I blinked, some of that silver would come off the lens and it was like having sand in my eyes. But it was the best they could do; that was 1957, and they didn't know that much about contact lenses. It was very, very painful.

What did you think of that film's floating brain prop?
  Oh, I thought it was terrible—just awful! They really could have done a heck of a lot better than that—it looked like a balloon with a face painted on it. And that's probably about what it was, too [*laughs*]! I can't really remember exactly what it was, I just know it was ludicrous.

How did you get along with Bert I. Gordon on Attack of the Puppet People?
  I don't know whether Bert Gordon liked me very much; we got into a little difficulty one night because he had promised me that I was only going to have to work until a certain hour. I was on a bowling team then and I was supposed to meet my wife and the team at such-and-such a time. Well, they carried me over past the time; Bert kept putting it off and putting it off, and I told him, "Look, you promised me I could be out of here by now, and you're foulin' me up!" I don't think he thought I was giving one hundred percent. *Puppet People* was half of a two-picture deal I had with American International; the other one was called *Jet Attack* [1958], with Audrey Totter. That *Puppet People* was kind of a nonsense picture.

Was it difficult working with Puppet People's *oversized props?*
  No, but that question reminds me of another time that Bert Gordon passed some kind of a comment. I had to climb a rope and pull myself up onto this giant table, and they were betting I couldn't do it. Bert Gordon was saying, "He'll never pull himself up there," and I said, "The hell I won't!" Don't tell me I can't do something, 'cause that's just when I'm going to go break my neck to prove I *can* do it. And I did it!

How much real guidance would an actor get from a director like Invisible Invaders' *Edward L. Cahn?*
  Edward Cahn was Mr. Speed-O; he'd jump up and almost get in the shot before he'd yell "cut"! But in all fairness I have to say that directors like Eddie Cahn didn't really have a chance. They had a schedule to contend with, and they wanted those films finished *ka-boom*. I think he did the best he could with the time he had, but in something like *Invisible Invaders* it's pretty much, "Learn the lines and get 'em out." They just didn't have the money to stay there and work on it.

Did you go to see all of your movies when they were first released?

A lot of the pictures I made were not released—they escaped [*laughs*]! I didn't avoid looking at them, but there were some where I knew full well what they were going to be like before they were ever released.

You've been directed by a lot of actors in your time—Abner Biberman, Edmond O'Brien, Hugo Haas and, on Hand of Death, *Gene Nelson. Did you ever think about directing a picture yourself?*

Well, I had a thought about doing it back then, and then I decided that I preferred to be in front of the camera rather than behind it. But the temptation was there for a time. Speaking of Gene Nelson, *Hand of Death* was his first shot at directing, and I thought he did a very good job for his first go at it.

Tell us a little about playing the monster in that film.

First they got some long johns and padded 'em to make me look like I weighed about four hundred pounds. Then they had this grotesque mask—a complete hood—and very large hands, to make me look burned. Our oldest boy, Martin, was maybe two or three years old at the time, and he came on the set with his mother and heard his dad's voice coming out of this monster get-up—and it scared him half to death! I had a tough time explaining it to him.

Was that an enjoyable change of pace, or was it too uncomfortable an experience?

Oh, no, it wasn't that bad—except at the very end, when I finally died. We went out to Malibu for a scene where I run into the ocean trying to get away from the police, and they shoot me. When I fell, the waves started knocking me around, and with that mask over my face I didn't know where I was! My eyes were set way back and the mask was sticking way out in front, and the only thing I could see was just directly straight out. I couldn't see the waves coming—that water was crashin' on me, and I was floppin' around, supposed to be dead [*laughs*]! That was quite an experience.

How did you get involved on Journey to the Seventh Planet?

A guy named Sidney Pink had made some kind of a deal to make that picture over in Denmark, and he contacted me about going over there and starring in it. He had already done one over there, a thing called *Reptilicus*—they showed it to me over in Denmark, and [*laughs*] I didn't think too much of it. Anyway, my wife and our son Martin went with me and enjoyed the trip very much. Something that I'll never forget is that when we flew from L.A., we went the Polar route and I got to see the North Lights—the Aurora Borealis. I think that was the most incredible thing I've ever seen. When we came back here, we went over to American International and we looped a great deal of that picture—almost all of it. I don't know what the trouble was, but American International wanted it all redubbed, so that's what we did.

Compared to The Brain from Planet Arous, *what did you think of* Seventh Planet's *giant brain prop?*

Actually, I believe that giant brain was done here, not in Denmark. The one in Denmark was worse than the one they did here [*laughs*]! They thought they could improve on it here, but as I remember it wasn't too good, either. So we did shoot some new shots for *Journey to the Seventh Planet* over here and they slipped a couple of 'em in.

Can you give us some background on the Larry Buchanan pictures you did in Texas?

What happened on those was that American International gave Larry Buchanan a budget to work with and scripts of pictures that they had already done. Larry, God bless him, is a nice guy but he really was not a director. He did the best he could, but he didn't even know enough not to "cross the line," which is one of the simplest things there is in directing. In the beginning, he didn't understand that [*laughs*]! The first picture I did for Larry was *Zontar, the Thing from Venus*; *Curse of the Swamp Creature* came next; then we did a war film called *Hell Raiders* [1968]. Of course I never thought those things would ever see the light of day—that was the only reason I did 'em!

You were working on actual locations most of the time, weren't you?

We did work mostly on location, although there were a couple of sets. We went out to Gordon McLendon's ranch on *Hell Raiders*; for *Zontar*, they used a park in Dallas, and we did work on a couple of stages in that. A lot of *Swamp Creature* was done in a little town called Uncertain, Texas—it was called that because the people who founded it weren't sure whether they were in Texas or Louisiana.

What about an obscure film called Night Fright, *made by many of the same people but not by Buchanan?*

I don't recall too much about that movie. It was produced by an attorney down there and directed by Jim Sullivan, who was an assistant director for Larry Buchanan.

How did you land your role in Dino De Laurentiis' King Kong?

I went out to Metro-Goldwyn-Mayer, read for it along with fifty other actors, and the director, John Guillermin, said he wanted me to do the part. But to this day I simply cannot understand why they wrote my scenes the way they did. Toward the end of the movie, Jeff Bridges and the others are running around New York wondering where Kong has gone, and then they realize that he'll think of the twin peaks and go to the World Trade Center. So Jeff Bridges calls me from out of the blue, but the audience doesn't know who in the heck I am. When King Kong was brought in and showed off, I was not in any of those scenes, and I never made contact with Jeff Bridges—but he calls me and puts all that trust in me. I never could understand that! My character was supposed to be a Jimmy Walker type of guy. Then at the very end, after Kong's been killed, they tried to show that I was really not concerned about the girl [Jessica Lange] or what she'd gone through, I was just trying to get publicity because I was a politician. But that scene didn't come off, either, and I knew it wouldn't. I just believe that, insofar as that character was concerned, they really weren't thinking. But, hey, I took the money and ran.

To most of us who enjoy the B-grade science fiction films of the '50s and '60s, your name seems synonymous with that type of entertainment. Do you appreciate or resent the association?
No, I don't resent being identified with them at all—why should I? Even though they were not considered top-of-the-line, for those people that like sci-fi I guess they were fun. My whole feeling about working as an actor is, if I give anyone any enjoyment, I'm doing my job, and that's what counts.

Considering the fact that you started out in first-rate pictures with people like John Ford and John Wayne, are you at all happy with the direction your career took?
Well, I think a lot of success was thrown at me too quickly and I wasn't ready to receive it. It was my fault if it didn't work out better; I can't blame anybody but myself.

How do you keep busy today?
I've been working with Brunswick Recreation Centers, with their Club 55 program, for the last few years. I travel around, kind of like a public relations guy, and try to get prime-timers—senior citizens—involved with the sport of bowling.

When you were making these sci-fi pictures twenty and thirty years ago, did you have any idea that they'd still be seen and appreciated in the 1980s?
[*Laughs*] Well, I don't know; you didn't think about those kinds of things at that time. They're making a lot of science fiction pictures nowadays that they don't call me about—maybe the fans appreciated me in these films, but the people in the business today certainly haven't said anything about me

doing any work for 'em. I think I have much more to offer as an actor now than I ever did as a young man; now would be a time for me to be a character actor. It hasn't worked out that way, but you never know what's going to happen. As long as there's breath in the body, I am still hopeful.

They Fought in the Creature Features
by Tom Weaver

[This interview followed the previous one by a few years, and now features some 21st century comments about *King Kong*]

IF ONE INDIVIDUAL were to be chosen as a poster boy for the science fiction movie boom of the 1950s and 1960s, that person should be John Agar. Typecast in the genre at the height of its popularity, he has appeared in more of that era's science fiction productions than any other actor, from favorites like *Revenge of the Creature* and *Tarantula* to notorious worst-film contenders like *The Brain from Planet Arous*, *Attack of the Puppet People* and *Curse of the Swamp Creature*.

Agar fought against this typecasting in the fifties, even walking away from a contract with a major studio (Universal-International) who saw him as their resident science fiction star. But Hollywood being what it is, he found himself back in the genre, time and again. If there was ever any bitterness on his part, it has apparently disappeared; he trades on the reputation now when he can, turning up with some regularity in newer science fiction films and thrillers and even appearing at science fiction conventions.

"If people want to see me, if they're interested in me, I'm more than happy to cooperate and get involved in things like that. Because the way I look at it, in essence the fan is really your boss, and they're the ones paying your salary [*laughs*]. But it does amaze me that there are people who like those sci-fi things we did thirty years ago and longer. *Tarantula*—the doggone thing is running on pay TV!"

Tall, lanky and always affable, Agar (now sporting a short white beard) is more than happy to swing down Memory Lane, pleased that the river of time has yet to sweep him downstream; the one question he is unable to answer, though, is just why people are still interested in John Agar. "For the life of me, I don't know! Last August [1989], I received a call from North Carolina, from a movie producer down there, Rick Brophy. A young man by the name of James Cummins wrote a script called *Winstrom*—it's a fantasy, big-budget film—and they want me to play the third lead in it. That's why I've got the beard. Originally they had Dennis Quaid and Meg Ryan playing the two leads, and I think they were going to do it through Fox. But then Fox wanted to take control and these people down in North Carolina didn't want 'em to, so I guess Fox is out. I don't know what the particulars are now, but they insist that I am to be in the movie.

"Today, unless you're box office and your name is current, if you go in for a part, you read for the producer or director. What amazed me was, these people in North Carolina wanted me to read the script and let them know if I wanted to do it [*laughs*]! That's something I just don't see that often anymore!"

Although *Winstrom* was never made, a steady string of recent movies *have* featured Agar in juicy supporting parts. The best known of this new bunch, *Miracle Mile*, did not set the 1989 box office on fire but got good word of mouth and enjoyed a second lease on life via pay television and videocassette. A sleeper about a group of Los Angeles nocturnal denizens reacting to news of an imminent nuclear strike, it featured Agar as Ivan Peters, grandfather of a coffee shop waitress (Mare Winningham) whose boyfriend (Anthony Edwards) inadvertently gets wind of the impending Armageddon. While Winningham and Edwards race to work out an escape plan, Agar and his wife, reconciling after years of separation, serenely drive to a restaurant for one last pleasant evening before The End comes. "*Miracle Mile*, I thought, was very well done. The writer-director Steve DeJarnatt—a very talented man—it took him ten years to get that picture into production, from the time when he first wrote the script. It was almost two years from the time they started to shoot before it was released. And then when they did release it, they released it at exactly the same time as *Batman*, *Ghostbusters II*, *Road House*—and it got lost."

Agar worked two weeks on the picture. "The two kids in it, Anthony Edwards and Mare Winningham, did a marvelous job. And then there was a gal from Texas, name of Lou Hancock, who played my wife, and I thought she also was wonderful in what she did. But, as I said, it got lost when it came out—partly, I think, because the subject matter of the film turned a lot of people off. But it's an exciting picture."

After years of battling monsters—the Creature from the Black Lagoon, the Mole People and Zontar, the Thing from Venus, to name a select few—Agar played a hermit who wanted to *become* a monster in director Clive Barker's *Nightbreed*, a 1990 release. "That was a strange situation. They had shot most of *Nightbreed* in England, and then they got to looking at the picture and in some ways it didn't make sense. The Nightbreed—some could be killed with gunfire, but some you could shoot and it wouldn't affect 'em at all. Some were affected by fire, and then with others, fire wouldn't affect them [*laughs*]. There was no explanation about any of this. So I think what happened was, somebody said, 'We better explain this thing,' so I came in and I did a scene with David Cronenberg, the Canadian director—this was his first big role in a movie. They had me tied in a chair with Christmas tree wires and bulbs while he tortures me. I was tied up for an hour and a half to two hours, sitting in that chair with that stuff wrapped around me—and then it took 'em 15 or 20 minutes to get it all off of me, they had it so tangled up [*laughs*]!"

An icon of sorts to fans of the older science fiction films, Agar liked working with modern genre giants Clive Barker and David Cronenberg, although he admits that he just barely got to know them in the one day it took to shoot his scenes. "Barker seemed to be a very nice man, and Cronenberg, too. Cronenberg chose to underplay his part; that was his choice, and Barker went with him. I think he underplayed it too much—too much for my taste, anyway. But that's a matter of opinion." Speaking of opinions, what did Agar think of the finished film? Not surprisingly, he reached the same conclusion as did the ticket-buying public, which stayed away in droves.

"Back when we made it, the only thing I saw were the scenes that I was in—I didn't read the script or anything. So I wanted to see what it was like. So I saw it—watched the whole thing. [*Shakes his head*] Uhn-uh. I pass. Didn't like the movie. They didn't go enough for story—it was just shock value.

"In all movies, I think the audience has the right to use their imagination. Today's pictures are just too graphic—they don't allow you to do that. Me, I won't go—rarely do I see a movie. I have cable, but I don't have any of the movie channels. There's a time and place for everything—we all go to the bathroom, but we don't need to photograph it."

A veteran of 50 films, Agar has been in the business since the late forties, when he signed a contract with Hollywood legend David O. Selznick. He never made a film for Selznick, but was lent to other producers and appeared in three of the decade's great action films—*Fort Apache*, *She Wore a Yellow Ribbon* and *Sands of Iwo Jima*—all opposite John Wayne. As a youth, however, acting—and career goals in general—were the farthest thing from John Agar's mind. "What would I have done if I hadn't gone into acting? To tell the truth, when I was growing up, I really, really hadn't any idea [*laughs*]! I used to play golf pretty well, and I might have gone in that direction—although I probably would have starved to death, the way Ben Hogan and guys like him played in those days."

The oldest of four children of a Chicago meat packer, Agar grew up during the Depression, although by dint of hard work his family remained upper middle class. "My dad used to go down to that stockyard and try to keep his meat packing company going. He had angina, and all this pressure put on him caused his early demise—he died before he reached his 41st birthday, and he left Mom loaded with four kids at the age of 38. I was 14—this was 1935."

After the death of his father, the Agars relocated to California, where in 1945 John found himself in the headlines when he become engaged to "America's Sweetheart," former child star Shirley Temple. Temple, who divorced Agar in 1949, wrote about the marriage in her 1988 book *Child Star: An Autobiography*, but Agar insists he has not read it.

"Another book, *Shirley Temple: America's Princess*, was written by a lady in Massachusetts; she had asked some questions of me about our marriage, and I told her flat out, 'What is personal in Shirley's life and personal in my life is nobody's business. And I'm not going to tell you anything.' When we were separated, we made an agreement, Shirley and I, that we would not say anything against each other. I kept that promise. I will continue to keep it. I'm never gonna say anything detrimental—that's the way it is." Has Shirley Temple held to that promise? "She broke the agreement as soon as we went into court," Agar deadpans. "But that's her problem, not mine."

While they were still husband and wife, the Agars appeared in two films together, the first of which, *Fort Apache* (1948), was Agar's debut as well as the first film in director John Ford's famous Cavalry Trilogy. "To me, John Ford was the epitome of screen directors. The first time I met Ford, he was on the same lot as David Selznick, who was my boss at the time—this was at RKO Pathe over in Culver City. I went in his office and he had me standing at attention and turning right face, left face. He said, 'Were you in the service?' and I said, 'Yes, sir. The Army Air Corps, sir.' 'Oh,' he said. 'You mean, off we go into the wild blue yonder—crash!' I said, 'Yes, sir. Were you in the service, Mr. Ford?' He said, 'Yep. The Navy.' I said, 'Oh, you mean, anchors aweigh—sink, huh?'

"So every time he would do something, I always considered he was kidding—and I'd kid him back! Duke, Hank Fonda, Ward Bond, Victor McLaglen, George O'Brien [the Ford regulars]—all these guys would say, 'We've know him for twenty-five, thirty years and we never know when he's kidding and when he's not.' But I always considered that he was kidding, and there's only one time I can remember that he really got mad at me [*laughs*]! He appeared tough, but I think Ford was a pussycat." Did Agar have first-picture nerves working with this giant of motion picture directors? "Listen, I was scared for the first twenty years." He laughs.

"You'd rehearse the scene before you'd shoot it, and John Ford wouldn't say a word to you. If you did the scene the way he thought it should be done, he still wouldn't say anything. And if you didn't do what he wanted, he would suggest [*softly*], 'Why don't you do *this*?' 'Why don't you do *that*?' Allan Dwan [*Sands of Iwo Jima*] was the same way. So was Jack Arnold [*Revenge of the Creature, Tarantula*]. Those were people who knew what they wanted. In fact, John Ford never went to rushes, and he never allowed actors to go. If everything was technically okay, Ford knew exactly what was on film.

He would go to the rough cut—that'd be the first time he'd see it. The only people who went to his rushes were the craft people. And the editor had only one way to cut that film—Ford's way—because that's all the film he had."

After a strong start, Agar's film career lost its momentum in the early fifties; in December 1950, he made his fantasy film debut playing the Scarlet Falcon in Columbia's *The Magic Carpet*, a Supercinecolor Arabian Nights programmer produced by low-budget legend Sam Katzman. "The Queen of Comedy, Lucille Ball, had a three-picture contract with Harry Cohn, who was the head of Columbia Pictures. She had made two pictures already [for $85,000 per film], and Cohn was trying to get out of having to make the third one. So he thought to himself, 'Well, I'll give her to Sam Katzman. He's making this movie called *The Magic Carpet*. She'll turn it down and I'll be out from under.' And Lucille Ball said, 'I'd *love* to do *The Magic Carpet*!' That movie took eighteen, maybe twenty days to shoot, and I don't think she worked over six—we were sitting there figuring out how much she was getting paid an hour! She was terrific, a lovely, wonderful lady."

Agar swashed and buckled his way through the film, dallied with harem beauties and even rode on the titular conveyance. "They had it on a platform, and then they had wires to make it take off. We were on a stage, and I was thirty feet in the air on this thing! Because of my body weight, I had to lean forward to keep it moving—otherwise it would jerk along, and they wanted a smooth ride. So we tried it and it jerked, and they said, 'You've got to lean forward *further*.' I did, and the thing tipped—you should have seen me hanging onto those wires, looking thirty feet down! That got my attention!"

Agar freelanced for a few years, showing up in the science fiction comedy *The Rocket Man* (scripted by Lenny Bruce) as well as in the Caribbean-made voodoo adventure *The Golden Mistress*. In 1954 Agar signed with Universal International, who were impressed with his work in *The Golden Mistress*. "I went under contract, and that was when I started into science fiction. I started out with *Revenge of the Creature*, the second Creature movie. We went to Florida, to Marineland, to shoot certain scenes, and that was lots of fun. There's one scene in there where Lori Nelson and I are swimming in a river, and that was done at Universal Studio in California. But all the underwater stuff was done in Florida. When the Creature grabbed Lori and carried her out of the Lobster House and I dove off the pier after them, that was in Florida, too. I remember there was a strong current in that river—when I dove in, it swept me quite a ways."

Swimming in the Marineland tank alongside its resident sharks did not faze Agar, Nelson or third lead John Bromfield. "In addition to Lori, John and myself, there was also Ricou Browning [the Creature], of course, and an underwater photographer. There might have been other people in there, too; in fact, I think some of the people who worked at Marineland were in the water with us, to keep creatures from getting into shots where they weren't wanted. We weren't really concerned about the sharks; Ricou was more concerned about the turtles. He had no peripheral vision at all while in that costume, and those dog-gone little suckers would come along and nip at him.

"Another thing that we were worried about were the moray eels—they hide in rock crevices and then jump out at you. That's the way they catch their dinner, by grabbing a fish or whatever comes by. They really weren't trouble, because we weren't about to go near the rocks where we knew they were hiding, but you could see their heads jumping out whenever a fish would go past." Plans to shoot scenes in the tank at night were discussed but quickly scuttled. "The people who were in charge said it wouldn't be a good idea. Those sharks were so well fed that you didn't have to worry about 'em during the daytime, but they didn't know what would happen at night."

When *Revenge of the Creature* made a splash at the box office, Universal was quick to place Agar in two other science fiction adventures, *Tarantula* and *The Mole People*. "The only picture that I made there that was not science fiction was *Star in the Dust* [1956], a Western. Then I got talking with them over there. I said, 'Gee, every time a science fiction picture comes along, you come after me.' They were building Rock Hudson and Tony Curtis at the time, and I wanted some of those kind of roles. But science fiction and the like was what they wanted me to do. So I said, 'Thanks a lot, but I'll go out on my own.'"

He made more money as a freelancer, but the reputation as a science fiction hero stuck as Agar waged war against the *Daughter of Dr. Jekyll*, *The Brain from Planet Arous* and *the Invisible Invaders*—as well as becoming a monster himself in *Hand of Death*. He hit rock bottom in the mid-sixties when he signed up to star in American International television movie remakes of the earlier AIPs *It Conquered the World*, *Voodoo Woman* and *Suicide Battalion*. "The director of those pictures, Larry Buchanan, was a man that was very involved with Sam Arkoff—AIP. They worked a deal where he could take some of the films that AIP had done previously, change 'em around and do 'em again for however much money. (I don't know what the price was, but believe me, it wasn't very much!) As far as I was concerned, that was just a way for me to make a little extra money—that's why I did 'em. Buchanan would fly me down to Texas, first-class accommodations, he met my salary—I had no kicks coming. Larry really was not a film director per se. He was learning his craft as we went along. I take my hat off to the guy, though—he tried. And from what I hear [*laughs*], he's still trying."

By the mid-sixties, the fifties-style science fiction films were out of vogue, and Agar busied himself in the supporting casts of various Westerns: *Stage to*

Thunder Rock, Law of the Lawless, Waco, the John Wayne vehicles *Chisum, Big Jake* and *The Undefeated* (from which Agar's footage was ultimately cut) and more. Film work was scarce in the seventies, with the notable exception of a cameo as the mayor of New York in Dino de Laurentiis's megabuck remake of *King Kong.*

"After I'd read for the role in *King Kong* and been accepted by [director] John Guillermin, I was told to go out to Metro at ten o'clock in the morning, to meet with Dino de Laurentiis. I get there quarter to ten, something like that, I'm sitting waiting, and all of a sudden Joyce Selznick, who is a casting lady and a niece of David's, says, 'Mr. de Laurentiis is not going to be able to keep the appointment.' I'd driven all the way from Burbank. She says, 'I'll call you later today, and we'll see if we can make it tomorrow.' So I go home, she calls me and says, 'All right, he can see you at ten o'clock tomorrow.'

"So I get out there again, about quarter to ten again, and about ten-fifteen he's ready to see me. Joyce takes me over to his office, we open the door, and I'll guarantee you, from the door to where his desk was, was a good forty feet—that's how deep it was. He's sitting there, and right next to him is a young man. Joyce introduces me to him, and then she introduces me to this young man, his son. That was it. He never said another thing. And I turned around and walked out. 'Hello, how are you?' 'Fine. How are you, sir?' And then I was ushered out. I went out there twice for that [*laughs*]!

"Out of curiosity, I went up to the top of the World Trade Center back then," he continued. "I wanted to see what it was like. I looked down at the King Kong they had built [the giant Kong body lying between the Twin Towers] and, oh my gosh, it was something! He was huge. Kong was so big that the people movin' around him looked like they were little mice! It was the first time I had ever been that high up, except in an airplane. The World Trade Center towers were the tallest buildings in the country, and it was truly remarkable to go up that high. It was just unbelievable, what [the 9/11 terrorists] did to those towers and to the Pentagon in Washington, D.C. And then the plane that crashed in Pennsylvania."

Having served on screen as its mayor, Agar remained wistful about New York City and optimistic about the future. "I truly hope it [the War on Terror] comes to an end so people stop going out and killing other people," he said. "It's about time that peace be worldwide. It has to end up that way sometime, because otherwise…the world is never, never gonna be right."

After some slow years, the offers are coming in again, and Agar is sifting through them, accepting the ones that "stick to my standards. I don't use four-letter words on the screen—no way." The thriller *Fear* with Ally Sheedy and *Perfect Bride* with Kelly Preston apparently met his criteria. "*Fear* is the story of a young lady [Sheedy] who is psychic. I play a psychopath. I've got a young girl tied up in the back of a car, and Sheedy's trying to convey to the police where we are. Eventually she does—I've taken this young lady to a barn, I've got her tied on the floor and I've got a pair of shears, rubbing 'em against her face. Four cops break in, but instead of giving up, I go over to the workbench and get a gun, and they shoot me."

That's when the fun started. "The special effects people had squibs on me and when the first one went off, I was going to hit the workbench with the lower part of my buttocks and throw myself up in the air. Then when the second squib went off, I was going to put my elbow on the workbench, roll off and fall to the ground. Well, I went up and my elbow missed. I hit hard—and I cracked my ribs. I wouldn't tell 'em—I wouldn't say a word. I was too embarrassed [*laughs*]! But I suffered for about three weeks after that."

Fear, directed by Rockne O'Bannon, premiered on cable television's Showtime rather than in theaters, but this bothers the self-effacing Agar about as much as the small size of his part. "To me, the idea of just working is what's fun. I don't give a doggone what kind of parts [I get]. Walter Huston said it years ago: 'I don't care about billing. If the show is good and I'm good in it, people are going to say, 'Who was that?' And if it's not, I don't want 'em to know I was in it!" [*laughs*]

And *Perfect Bride*? "That stars a gal by the name of Sammi Davis—an English actress—and Kelly Preston, who was in *Twins* [1988]. I play a ninety-year-old grandpa in this one; a friend of mine, an actor by the name of John Larch, said, 'Don't worry, Agar. They got makeup, they can tone ya down.' [*laughs*] Sammi plays a nurse, and in her childhood, her mother was mistreated by her father. It did something to her way of thinking, and now any time she comes in contact with anybody (especially a man) that she thinks is doing her wrong, she takes a syringe and sticks it in their neck, and they appear to die of a heart attack. Now, she is engaged to my grandson. Kelly Preston is my granddaughter, and she becomes suspicious of Sammi. Everything was done on location, we shot over in West L.A., just off of Washington Boulevard. I had a good time doing it." (*Perfect Bride* also went directly to TV and videocassette.)

The careers of B movie stars do not often have happy endings, but John Agar is delighted to find that he has become an exception to that rule. "Acting is something that I love to do, but it's a part of me that's often dormant. So when I get an opportunity to go on a set, it's like somebody's pushing a button that's been idle for a long time. And right away, I'm ready to get going at it. It's fun for me to be able to get back into it, because it's a part of my life that I've really enjoyed."

BearManorMedia
PO BOX 71426 · ALBANY, GEORGIA 31708

THE PHILIP RAPP JOKE FILE
For the first time ever, be privy to the open caverns of mirth that is the prolific Philip Rapp joke file! Rapp, writer for Baby Snooks, Eddie Cantor and creator of the *Bickersons*, wrote and collected jokes for years, drawing from it during his classic radio and TV years. Now we've taken the best quips and put them together for one great and funny book! Illustrated.
ISBN: 1-59393-102-6. $14.95

NOT SO DUMB
THE LIFE AND CAREER OF MARIE WILSON
by Charles Tranberg
Ready for the first biography on blonde, bubbly Marie Wilson? Was she really that vapid? Well — read the book on this *My Friend Irma* star!
ISBN: 1-59393-049-6. $19.95

TWENTY QUESTIONS
by Robert VanDeventer
A novelized memoir of *Twenty Questions*, one of the first weekly panel quiz shows on the radio.
ISBN: 1-59393-077-1. $19.95

INCORRECT ENTERTAINMENT
by Anthony Slide
Cultural Historian Anthony Slide, who has been described by the *Los Angeles Times* as a one-man publishing phenomenon, strikes again with a book guaranteed to contain something OFFENSIVE for everyone. From FASCISM in Hollywood to the latest topical jokes on the *Challenger* disaster & more.
ISBN: 1-59393-093-3. $19.95

FRED MACMURRAY: A BIOGRAPHY
by Charles Tranberg
A biography of Hollywood's most famous dad! Features an introduction by Don Grady of *My Three Sons*. Coming in October!
ISBN: 1-59393-099-2. $24.95.

ANGELIC HEAVEN
A Fan's Guide To Charlie's Angels
by Mike Pingel
The ultimate fan's guide to the hit 70s/80s television series by legendary producer Aaron Spelling. Filled with facts about the show, behind-the-scenes tidbits, rare photos and forewords by Farrah Fawcett and Cheryl Ladd, Angelic Heaven will have you rushing out to buy the DVDs!
$19.95

WHO'S WHO OF STAGE & SCREEN
by C. Elizabeth Lalla
Who's Who of Stage and Screen will make a beautiful addition to any Hollywood lover's collection! Filled with photos, profiles, resumes and contact information for the artists included. Nearly 600 pages, 8x10 size!
$35.00

THE FILMS OF THE DIONNE QUINTUPLETS
by Paul Talbot
An emphasis on their interesting film career of the famous five. Packed with photos and priceless information, every film fan will marvel at their story. Ships in August.
ISBN: 1-59393-097-6. $19.95.

ADD $3.00 POSTAGE FOR EACH BOOK

ORDER THESE BOOKS AND MORE! VISIT WWW.BEARMANORMEDIA.COM

www.ingramcontent.com/pod-product-compliance
Lightning Source LLC
Chambersburg PA
CBHW071626170426
43195CB00038B/2141